KAUTO STAR

A Steeplechasing Legend

KAUTO STAR

A Steeplechasing Legend

edited by ANDREW PENNINGTON
with an introduction by ALICE PLUNKETT

RACING POST

First published in Great Britain in 2012 by
Racing Post Books, Axis House, Compton, Newbury, Berkshire, RG20 6NL

10 9 8 7 6 5 4 3 2 1

A catalogue record for this book is available from the British Library.

ISBN 978-1-908216-45-8

Designed by Soapbox
www.soapbox.co.uk

Printed and bound in the UK by Butler, Tanner and Dennis, Frome

www.racingpost.com/shop

Contents

Introduction

by Alice Plunkett

Channel 4 Racing

AS A RACING FAN I feel unbelievably privileged to have been able to appreciate the age of Kauto Star. Is he the best ever? Is he greater than Arkle? I don't honestly know, and I'm not sure that I really care, because for eight glorious seasons I have marvelled at his brilliance, bravery and exuberance, his quality and elegance, at times his fallibility, but most of all his longevity.

Training horses day in, day out makes you realise they are possibly second only to sheep in their ability to injure themselves. They are brilliant at finding the sharp edge, the hole in the field, the one rough bit of ground or stone to stand on to give them the injury that rules them out of their intended engagement.

Kauto Star has been masterfully produced at the top of his game year in, year out by trainer Paul Nicholls and his team in Ditcheat to appear at seven consecutive Cheltenham Festivals. Even before taking in what he does when he performs, the mere fact we have all had the opportunity to build such a relationship with him over so many years has added to the emotive nature of his story.

Of course we marvel at the brilliance of Frankel, a freak of a beast who demolishes his opposition with consummate ease. Crowds flock to see him for the 'I was there' moment. The difference, though, with jump racing and Kauto Star is that for the best part of a decade we have built a relationship with him.

Each October at the start of the season is like catching up with an old school friend. We know all there is to know about his regime, his trainer and groom, the highs and lows and what could go wrong, but as each year has passed the anxiety has grown with every run as the attachment and friendship builds stronger and stronger.

By the time of the Cheltenham Gold Cup of 2012 the feelings had become so strong that when the great Ruby Walsh pulled up Kauto Star on the first circuit the spontaneous applause that rung around the racecourse summed up in a moment where this horse lay in the racing public's heart. There was no concern for a losing bet or prize money lost, only that their dear friend was coming back from the battle safe and sound for whatever Nicholls and his owner Clive Smith planned for him in the future.

Looking back over the eight seasons of his career in Britain, Kauto Star has given all of us on Channel 4 Racing so many truly great moments to cover. He has provided a rhythm and focus to the jumps seasons and a genuine reason to reach for the superlatives. Often in journalism we hype the average, but with him we have had the genuine opportunity to get completely carried away!

There have been so many pieces to the jigsaw that makes his story: the characters around him, his stablemate and fellow star Denman, the slightly rollercoaster start to his career in Britain, his last-fence blunders, his versatility, as well as the tremendous access we have been given to him by his connections.

These characters are led by seven-time champion trainer Paul Nicholls and his able deputies, Dan Skelton and Clifford Baker. Paul is arguably the most accessible champion trainer jump racing has had. His patience and amenability with the increasing desire for more information and more access has been extraordinary.

He has masterminded the careers of the two horses of our generation with a generosity that has added to the pure pleasure of the brilliance of Denman and Kauto Star. I don't even want to count the number of times I have phoned him to ask for another pre-King George or pre-Cheltenham Festival visit with the cameras or to ask him to appear on a Cheltenham preview night panel.

The highlight of all the features I have done was being Kauto Star's groom for two days. It is bizarre how, despite the fact I have mucked out horses all my life, cleaning out Kauto's stable felt a privilege. There is the strict routine to his morning that Rose Loxton, his groom, explained to me. He is in a small yard next to Denman, Master Minded and Big Buck's – i.e. Millionaires' Row – but he gets everything first.

Riding out alongside him with his daily work-rider Clifford Baker in the saddle felt like meeting Roger Federer or Usain Bolt, Sir Alex Ferguson or David Beckham. I am not humanising Kauto, he just has that aura that people who are the best at what they do have. He cruised up Nicholls' steep gallop effortlessly, relishing the routine that was certainly not for the faint-hearted. I was blown away by how fresh and enthusiastic he was for another day's work.

Clifford Baker has been a key part of Kauto's success because he has ridden him pretty well every day of his time at Ditcheat, and alongside his various grooms has constantly monitored his wellbeing – morning, noon and night. Clifford can read Kauto like a book, whether on his back or in his unique stable habits.

I always love chatting to him about the horse, as he is the consummate professional but feels so lucky to be associated with this horse of a lifetime. His wife rang me before his 50th birthday to see if Highflyer could make a DVD of all the features and races of Kauto's career that we had in the archive. Of course we were thrilled to help. Poor Sarah, I think, now regrets making that request, as when Clifford is not out with Kauto on the yard he is spending his evenings watching him on the television!

Irish champion jockey Ruby Walsh has also been an integral part of the story. He was convinced Kauto Star would cope with a step up in trip ahead of his first Betfair Chase win in November 2006; he defended his charge and ironed out his last-fence jumping blunders. For me, Ruby has almost been as brilliant on the horse in defeat as he has in victory, but the rhythm they get into around Kempton is the standout feature of their partnership.

I have loved the dynamic between Denman and Kauto too. Several summers when they are out in the field on their holidays with Big Buck's and Master Minded I have been down to see them. Denman is absolutely the alpha male in the group, completely dominating the others. The thought has often occurred to me whether this dominance would ever transfer itself onto the racecourse. If Denman were leading and Kauto went to pass him, would he ever be intimidated as he seems to be in the field and back away from him?

That clearly has never been the case as, and the two have mostly been kept apart other than in the Gold Cup, when it has been each man for himself. That said, their differences and their closeness has added to the scenario. Denman 'The Tank', Kauto the athlete.

Clive Smith is arguably the luckiest man in jump racing. To have both Master Minded and Kauto Star in your colours is a dream that he has had the opportunity to live. This book lets him and all of us relive the wonderful ride we have all been on with Kauto and his team through the *Racing Post*'s unrivalled coverage of his illustrious career.

We all have our favourite Kauto moment that will feature here. For me, his Haydock success in the autumn of 2011 was right up there, as it was so unexpected. Andrew Franklin, the brilliant executive producer of Channel 4 Racing, had felt it was the last time we would genuinely be able to build the old horse up. Our whole programme was devoted to footage of his entire career: it felt almost like an obituary! The horse was applauded from the saddling boxes, into and around the paddock and down to post.

Donna Blake, Nicholls' travelling head groom was nearly crying legging up Ruby, and by the time the race started it felt like mild hysteria was spreading round the racecourse. This reached fever pitch as it became clear that Kauto had them all on the stretch going into the second circuit, including the reigning Gold Cup hero Long Run – and Kauto stormed all the way to the line to a reception the like of which I have never heard before. As I walked into the winner's enclosure with him interviewing Ruby we passed seasoned racegoers in tears. Three cheers rang out around the winner's enclosure, and Paul Nicholls nearly burst with pride.

The *Racing Post* writers are much more eloquent than me at describing the innumerable highs we have all shared thanks to Kauto Star, so enjoy dipping into your highlights of the treasure of jump racing of this century.

1

French beginnings

Previous spread: Kauto Star en route to victory on his final start in France at Auteuil, 30 May 2004

Below: Serge Foucher, who trained and part-owned Kauto Star in France

THE KAUTO STAR STORY began not in Somerset with Paul Nicholls, but in France. In an extraordinary tale from straight out of a novel, it was bloodstock agent Anthony Bromley who was responsible for bringing Kauto to Britain, as Peter Thomas discovered.

Any unsuspecting Brit who has been caught in a stationary pari-mutuel queue at Longchamp or a ten-mile tailback of revolting lorry drivers at Dover docks will know that doing business with the French can be hard work. The normal rules of engagement don't always apply where our Gallic cousins are involved, and what looked on the surface like a done deal can turn into a good deal more than was bargained for.

Many a nice horse has passed across the Channel in recent years to grace the British jump racing arena, but a lot of them have come accompanied by tales of crisis and complication. None, however, can have featured in such a saga of confusion as the mighty Kauto Star, the one-time crazy horse who, despite the best efforts of himself and his trainer, ended up on a lorry bound for King George and Gold Cup glory.

For Anthony Bromley, the man who has made a habit of liberating the best bloodstock the country has to offer, meeting with a little French resistance was nothing new, but even he was left bemused by the lengths to which this horse's trainer was prepared to go to keep him at home.

The tale began with a hat-trick of hurdling victories for the three-year-old son of Village Star at Enghien and Auteuil in the spring and autumn of 2003. Bromley's far-reaching grapevine of continental contacts ensured that Kauto Star was brought to his notice, but at this stage his interest didn't extend as far as naming a price.

The prolific purchaser of champions takes up the story: 'Because of those early successes, he couldn't run in races like the Triumph Hurdle, because he wouldn't qualify as a novice, so we showed only a cursory interest in him that season. Anyway, although he'd won three in a row to start off with, after that, through the winter and the

spring of 2004, he'd always come up short behind an amazing filly called Maia Eria in the top races.

'But physically he was starting to grow and we found from his trainer, Serge Foucher, that he'd been coughing through the winter and that was perhaps why he hadn't been at his best at the start of his four-year-old campaign.

'Serge was starting to get excited by the time early May came around and all the little problems had disappeared, but it was still a bit of a surprise when he came out and won the Grade 3 for four-year-olds on Grand Steeple-Chase weekend at Auteuil at 36-1. Maia Eria was probably over the top that day and could only finish fifth, but the race had been truly run and the form seemed to stack up. That was when he started to become of real interest to us.'

Foucher was, indeed, becoming excited, to the point where he gushingly described Kauto Star as 'l'extraterrestrial', a remark easily translated by even the slowest Brit, and one the trainer would soon

Kauto Star winning for the first time in his career at Enghien, 14 April 2003

come to regret. The horse was now well and truly on Bromley's ever-blinking radar and a deal was nigh.

The only trouble for our man was that Foucher, far from being just the horse's minder, in fact owned half of him. What's more, he was in no mood to part with 50 per cent of an animal he believed to be possessed of championship potential. He would later tell a tale of the day a prospective buyer came to view Kauto Star as a mad-as-a-hatter, maverick two-year-old, only to be felled by a kick to the head that left him flat on his back with all the appearance of being stone dead. Clearly, neither part-owner nor horse was going to go without a fight.

Luckily for Bromley, where there is a trainer with a half-share, there is another half-shareholder who is not a trainer and is less likely to be defiantly resistant to a reasonable offer, and that man soon made himself known.

'The trainer wasn't normally a seller,' explains Bromley, 'but David Powell, our French agent, rang on the Monday after the Auteuil race and said the other half-owner, Claude Cohen, had let it be known he would be interested in selling for the right money. No figures were mentioned, but it was then that we started to get to work.'

He adds: 'There had been excuses for previous failures and the horse looked so well and seemed to be springboarding forward at such a rate that on the Tuesday I had the video couriered to Clive Smith. Clive had recently been the underbidder when JP McManus bought Garde Champetre for 530,000gns, so it seemed natural to offer this new horse to him.

'We knew other French agents were sniffing around, so we made an offer on the Wednesday and the deal was agreed on the Thursday, which just left the routine vetting procedure.'

If ever the word 'routine' was sorely misplaced, this was the time. In fairness, Bromley anticipated that things might not go with silky smoothness and organised for both himself and Powell to accompany Highflyer's vet, Buffy Shirley-Beavan, to the little village training centre of Senonnes. In the event, he would have done well to take along Sherlock Holmes as well.

'We were concerned about the reception Buffy might get,' says Bromley, 'and David was there just in case we needed any serious French spoken, but when we got there, we were glad to find that

Opposite: Kauto Star glides over a hurdle at Auteuil on his last start in France, 30 May 2004

Serge was being quite pleasant. It was lunchtime, so the place was quiet, but he got Kauto Star out on the gallops on his own and let Jerome Guiheneuf, his regular jockey, put him through his paces.

'Everything was going fine, so we went back to the yard, where Buffy was going to scope him to check his larynx and make sure he hadn't bled. It was the last part of the jigsaw, but the horse flatly refused to accept the scope up his nostrils, no matter how hard we tried.

'The jockey was half-chuckling as he explained to us: "We knew you wouldn't be able to do that because we've never been able to."

'Buffy suggested that as a last resort we could dope him – not perfect, but it would get the job done – but when we looked round to find Serge to get his permission, we realised that once we'd come off the gallops he'd disappeared, leaving his mobile phone behind, into the depths of the French countryside.'

It may not have been subtle, but it was effective. With no trainer, there would be no permission, and with no permission, no scope, which would turn any purchase into a dangerous game. Foucher's wife tried frantically to contact him, trying all the places she thought he might have gone, but he was nowhere to be found.

A plan to run Kauto Star in a big race a couple of weeks later made the scoping a matter of urgency, but the eager buyers were left high and dry. On the way back to the airport, however, Bromley called both Smith and Paul Nicholls and explained the situation to them, that the horse hadn't been scoped but that he had been running well and looked great. Smith, with his characteristic bullshit-busting approach, led the way.

'You've got to be extremely lucky,' says the world's luckiest owner, 'but I always like to see a horse who wants to get on with it, and when I see that, I make a decision very quickly, whereas I think some people overcomplicate things.

'It might be nice to get a bit more involved, but there's very often a sense of urgency with these deals, so you have to make your mind up quickly and get things settled before someone else steps in.

'I've got to know Anthony well and we've developed a trust and confidence that makes it easy for us to do business. I try to give him a proper decision very, very quickly – there will be negotiation over the price, but we're working on it very quickly – and I think sellers like that.'

After a decisive council of war, the decision was made to buy Kauto Star and the courtesy phone call was put in to Foucher, who had by this time been reunited with his mobile and was about to receive the news he hadn't wanted to hear: his extraterrestrial was on his way to Blighty for €400,000. He wasn't a happy lapin.

Bromley says: 'At this point, he completely lost the plot and started banging on about how we couldn't buy the horse without vetting him completely. He got very upset.

'You had to feel for him in a way. At four, this horse had gone from looking okay to being a potential champion, and poor Serge was well aware of that. I hadn't bought a horse from him before and haven't since, but there are no hard feelings from us. I'm sure every trainer in England would sympathise with him, especially since we found that his wife left him a couple of months after the horse was sold.'

Nobody felt sorrier for Foucher than Bromley, but business was business and, six days after Kauto Star had revealed his full potential at Auteuil, he was in Smith's ownership and heading for Ditcheat, where he would rise to the top of the steeplechasing tree.

For Bromley, it was another job well done and another saga ended. He reflects: 'We couldn't have predicted he would be the phenomenon he turned out to be, but he certainly ticked a lot of the boxes for us. He'd only won four from ten in France, so it required a bit of a leap of faith to buy him, especially as, at the time, he was the most expensive horse I'd ever bought, but when you like a horse the way we liked him, sometimes you have to take a chance.

'I think the reason we have done so well in France is that our investors trust us enough to let us act quickly for them. It's very often not a simple matter. You have to move quickly and be prepared to go with the flow.'

Kauto Star entered the care of Paul Nicholls, a trainer who was at the top of his game, and it was clear – not just from the €400,000 purchase price – that the Ditcheat handler had an exciting prospect on his hands. By the end of 2004, and approaching Kauto's fifth birthday, the wraps were taken off and the horse was introduced to the racing public in Britain.

2

Making his mark

Previous spread: Kauto Star and Ruby
Walsh make a winning British debut at
Newbury, 29 December 2004

Right: Jayne Sleep on Kauto Star as
he settles into Paul Nicholls' yard

KAUTO STAR HAD CLEARLY settled in well into his new surroundings and he was the subject of positive noises from the West Country before his eagerly awaited debut at Newbury. As Seb Vance reported, on the racecourse he made an immediate impression.

A machine was how Ruby Walsh described Kauto Star following an impressive British debut and bookmakers quickly took note, some firms making the youngster as low as 5-1 favourite for the Arkle Trophy at the Cheltenham Festival.

Clive Smith's four-year-old, who had been placed in Grade 1 events at Auteuil in France, was the focus of some bullish reports from trainer Paul Nicholls beforehand. As a result, he was sent off 2-1 joint-favourite with Irish Champion Hurdle winner Foreman, who was also making his chasing debut.

The race panned out as the betting suggested and there is every chance the pair could reoppose at the festival.

Nicholls said: 'He was bought to jump fences and the first time he schooled he jumped brilliantly. Ruby got off and said he was a machine. End of story.'

The Arkle, for which Kauto Star is as big as 8-1 with VCbet among others, is a 'consideration'.

Kauto Star's potential was neatly summed up by Bruce Jackson in his race analysis: 'Connections are looking forward to developing him as a Gold Cup contender for the future, sure that he will get the longer trip, and he looks to have a bright future.'

After second favourite Fundamentalist was ruled out of the Arkle the following month, Kauto Star was clear favourite for the race, and he had progressed physically further, according to Nicholls, before his second start at Exeter.

However, Kauto made front page news in the Racing Post *after he was beaten into second due to Ruby Walsh's decision to remount after falling at the second-last fence. This sparked a full-scale debate on remounting, but two days later Kauto's season was over, as Jon Lees reported:*

NEWBURY, 29 December 2004			
Western Daily Press Club Novices' Chase		2m2½f	
1	Kauto Star	2-1jf	R Walsh
2	Foreman	2-1jf	AP McCoy
3	Sleep Bal	7-1	M Fitzgerald
8 ran 9l, 15l			

EXETER, 31 January 2005			
Weatherbys Bank Novices' Chase		2m1½f	
1	Mistral De La Cour	20-1	A Thornton
2	Kauto Star	2-11f	R Walsh
PU	Goldbrook	6-1	T Scudamore
3 ran sh hd			

Kauto Star, ante-post favourite for the Arkle Trophy, was ruled out for the rest of the season last night after he was found to have suffered a fracture to a hind leg.

The injury was discovered in x-rays taken after the novice chaser ran at Exeter on Monday, when he fell but was remounted by Ruby Walsh to take second after contesting a driving finish.

Announcing the news, trainer Paul Nicholls described the injury as 'not major', but serious enough to keep him off the track until next season. Kauto Star was one of his leading candidates for Cheltenham Festival honours, having created a huge impression when winning on his British debut at Newbury in December.

He still headed the betting for the Arkle even after Monday's mishap in a race that led to calls for the practice of remounting fallers to be outlawed.

Nicholls added: 'Kauto Star was stiff and sore after his race on Monday and for my peace of mind I decided to have him x-rayed this afternoon. It showed a small fracture to his near-hind leg. It's not major, but enough to keep him out for the season.

'I've spoken to his owner and we have no option but to box-rest him until he's over his injury and that's it for the season. It's very disappointing, as he would have had a big chance in the Arkle, but we've still got a horse for the future.'

Kauto Star was given three months' box rest before being turned out to grass. Nicholls was pleased with his progress by the autumn, saying in October: 'We are all very excited about him and the sky's the limit. He's done plenty of schooling at home and his jumping has been superb.'

He reappeared in the Haldon Gold Cup at Exeter, but it was the death of triple Cheltenham Gold Cup winner Best Mate that made the headlines. In the race itself, Kauto Star finished a four-length second to Monkerhostin, after which assistant trainer Dan Skelton said: 'He'll improve one hell of a lot for that.'

For his next start, when he stepped into Grade 1 company in Britain for the first time in the Tingle Creek at Sandown Park, Kauto Star had to do without the injured Ruby Walsh. With Mick Fitzgerald in the saddle, he put up a superlative performance, as Lee Mottershead reported:

EXETER, 1 November 2005		
William Hill Haldon Gold Cup Chase (Limited handicap)	2m1½f	
1 Monkerhostin	10-1	R Johnson
2 Kauto Star	3-1	R Walsh
3 Ashley Brook	7-4f	P Brennan
11 ran 4l, 9l		

Kauto Star with Paul Nicholls' wife Georgie

Take a journey back in time. Return yourself to the Tingle Creek Trophy of 12 months ago, a race that Azertyuiop was 5-6 favourite to win for Paul Nicholls.

Back then, stablemate Kauto Star had not raced in Britain, nor run for Nicholls, nor even jumped a fence in public.

Since then he has romped home at Newbury, shot to Arkle Trophy favouritism, fractured a leg at Exeter, and spent months convalescing. And since then he has also done what the now-sidelined Azertyuiop could not. He has won the Tingle Creek. There are two great races

Kauto Star and Mick Fitzgerald race clear of Ashley Brook in the Tingle Creek at Sandown, 3 December 2005

Right: Kauto Star and his delighted connections in the winner's enclosure at Sandown

SANDOWN, 3 December 2005		
William Hill Tingle Creek Trophy Chase		2m
1 Kauto Star	5-2jf	M Fitzgerald
2 Ashley Brook	5-2jf	AP McCoy
3 Oneway	4-1	G Lee
7 ran 1½l, 8l		

for two-mile chasers. Kauto Star has won one of them and is now favourite with many bookmakers to win the other. The absent Moscow Flyer, whose William Hill Tingle Creek crown Kauto Star took, has been deposed as the Champion Chase 'jolly' with both Totesport and Ladbrokes, the latter being most impressed by Kauto Star. They make him 2-1 favourite from 7-2, and anyone thinking of backing the horse should be encouraged by this – the best is yet to come.

It surely must be. The horse who gave Hennessy hero Mick Fitzgerald his second consecutive big Saturday win is a novice in all but name.

This was only his fourth run over fences, he hated the ground, and he wants to race left-handed. But despite all that, he did what you have to do in the breathless frenzy of a Tingle Creek – he jumped magnificently, and particularly so over the often crucial railway fences.

'It's all very well having potential and belief, but you've got to do it, and he's gone and done it,' said Nicholls, who was landing his third Tingle Creek after the wins of Flagship Uberalles (1999) and Cenkos (2002).

'I had two targets in mind for him,' Nicholls added.

'One was to try to win this, and the other is to try to win the Champion Chase. This is a young horse, he keeps galloping and is going to keep improving. He's learning and is relaxing. He has class, that's what he's got.'

That class was evident in the way Clive Smith's charge cruised through the contest. An encouraging second on his Haldon Gold Cup return, he travelled easily behind leader Ashley Brook before Fitzgerald sent him ahead at the pond fence. His stamp on the proceedings was immediate and, though he idled when clear on the run-in, the antics were merely a sign that he is still little more than a baby, and a baby who would rather not go right-handed. Happily, Cheltenham is left-handed.

'He goes a little bit left and is a little bit green in front,' said Nicholls, who, when asked to compare Kauto Star with his 2004 Champion Chase winner Azertyuiop, revealed: 'My head groom Clifford Baker rides him at home, and I asked him that the other day. He said he compares favourably, but they are different horses.'

Kauto Star will definitely be aimed at the Game Spirit Chase at Newbury. Nicholls will not mind if that is the youngster's only race before Cheltenham, where Fitzgerald is adamant a better horse will be seen.

'He jumped superbly,' said Fitzgerald, 'but he hated the ground and will definitely be better left-handed. He's a lovely horse but I'm only keeping the seat warm for Ruby.

'I bet Ruby was at home looking at the race and thinking, "Where is he going?" I've actually given him what I consider a bad ride.

'Ruby told me – and even Paul said – not to get into a battle and turn it into a real slog.

'The problem with him is that he's such a good traveller and such a good jumper, I kept thinking 'we're not going fast enough'. I thought, 'I'm breaking his stride by stopping him all the time'.

'He'll be even better when he goes left-handed, and he's a proper Champion Chase horse.'

Ruby is a lucky man indeed.

Kauto Star and Clifford Baker (left)
with his stablemates at Ditcheat

*The Game Spirit Chase in early February would have been Kauto Star's
prep race for the Champion Chase, but Newbury was claimed by frost
and he did not have another race before the festival.*

*In the run-up to Cheltenham Nicholls told Ben Newton how
important his new star was: 'Kauto is the one that really matters. I
can honestly say that, out of all my Cheltenham runners this year, he
is the one who, from the moment he came back into training, has had
everything geared towards winning at the festival.'*

*Head groom Clifford Baker expressed his confidence in the stable star:
'I've been fortunate enough to have ridden See More Business, Azertyuiop
and Kauto Star in most of their work, and Kauto is right up there. See
More Business was more of a stayer, while Azertyuiop had amazing toe
over the first couple of furlongs, but Kauto Star slots nicely into the middle.
To be a champion two-mile chaser you need speed and the ability to stay,
and he has a perfect blend of the two. I'll stick with him as my banker.'*

*Everything went to plan in the build-up, but everything did not go to
plan in the race itself, as Tony Smurthwaite reported:*

Kauto Star crashed out after three fences in a dramatic running of
the Queen Mother Champion Chase, but the 2-1 favourite may be
asked to atone at Aintree.

Paul Nicholls and Ruby Walsh after Kauto Star fell in the Queen Mother Champion Chase at Cheltenham, 15 March 2006

Thierry Majorcryk had already been unseated from French mare Kario De Sormain after the first when Kauto Star failed to take off and crashed into the third fence, hampering Moscow Flyer and bringing down Dempsey.

Trainer Paul Nicholls said: 'He's fine and lives to fight another day. Maybe his slight inexperience at this level has just caught him out. He seems okay and could now go to Aintree. As he is only six, he has plenty more chances ahead of him.'

Kauto Star was bruised and sore in the aftermath of the Champion Chase and did not run again that season. Hopes were high that he would continue his development. Exciting times lay ahead.

CHELTENHAM, 15 March 2006		
Queen Mother Champion Chase		2m
1 Newmill	16-1	A McNamara
2 Fota Island	4-1	AP McCoy
3 Mister McGoldrick	50-1	D Elsworth
F Kauto Star	2-1f	R Walsh
12 ran 9l, 1½l		

3

At the summit

THE SEASON WHICH would end with a £1 million bonus wrapped in gold began with Nicholls expressing his hope that Kauto Star would be better over further than two miles, and he was duly entered for the King George VI Chase at Kempton on Boxing Day.

The first port of call, however, was Aintree and a first start over two and a half miles over fences in the Old Roan Chase. Nicholls expected him to improve for the run, but Kauto was more than ready, as Colin Russell reported:

Kauto Star soared to the head of the King George VI Chase betting yesterday when sauntering to victory at Aintree, eclipsing the memory of his fall at Cheltenham in March.

The Paul Nicholls-trained star is now 7-2 favourite with sponsors Stan James for the 3m Boxing Day feature at Kempton, despite never having raced beyond 2m4f.

That fact also failed to stop bookmakers from speculating on Clive Smith's six-year-old stepping up even further in trip and contesting the 2007 Totesport Cheltenham Gold Cup.

William Hill and bet365 both introduced Kauto Star at 10-1 for that race, while he is as short as 5-2 favourite for the Champion Chase with Hills.

Brilliant is an overused adjective, but it was a highly appropriate one to describe Kauto Star's performance yesterday after he had trounced his rivals in the Grade 2 Bonusprint.com Old Roan Chase.

Having his first run since falling at the third when favourite for last season's Champion Chase and his first over 2m4f, Kauto Star carried top weight to a scintillating success over Armaturk and Inca Trail.

The distances were 21 lengths and eight lengths, but those bare facts fail to do justice to a memorable performance.

Nicholls, who watched the contest from Wincanton, said: 'Obviously I'm delighted he has jumped so well and won the way

AINTREE, 22 October 2006			
Bonusprint.com Old Roan Chase 2m4f (Limited handicap)			
1	Kauto Star	evens f	R Walsh
2	Armaturk	13-2	J Maguire
3	Inca Trail	12-1	G Lee
5 ran 21l, 8l			

A giant leap from Kauto Star during the Old Roan Chase at Aintree, 22 October 2006

he did over the two and a half miles, which opens up plenty more options for us this season.

'My first thoughts are to aim him at the King George at Kempton on Boxing Day, and he is likely to have only one more run between now and then. That could be in the Tingle Creek at Sandown.'

Nicholls' assistant Dan Skelton, supervising the yard's runners at Aintree, added: 'Ruby was delighted with that. It was a great start to his season. He showed he definitely stays and he confirmed what we've always thought, that he's a very good horse. Paul has always held him in the highest regard.

'He jumped brilliantly, settled well, and, in giving 9lb and a 21-length beating to Armaturk, it was a top-class performance.'

In his first column for the Racing Post *a week later Nicholls revealed he was 'thinking about' an assault on the Cheltenham Gold Cup and added that the Betfair Chase was the preferred stepping-stone to the King George on Boxing Day.*

The step up to three miles would not be a problem, according to Nicholls, who said: 'I honestly think he will [stay] and Clifford Baker has always said he'd be top-class from two miles to three miles.'

And in the Betfair Chare at Haydock Park, Kauto Star was a class apart, as Tom O'Ryan reported:

Forget talk of him being over-hyped. Dismiss suggestions of him being a doubtful stayer. Instead, reflect on a performance which bore all the hallmarks of a class act. Put succinctly, Kauto Star, stepping up to 3m for the first time in his fledgling career, was nothing less than poetry in motion in the Betfair Lancashire Chase, leaving nobody in any doubt that they had witnessed the ascent of a rapidly soaring star.

'Awesome' was the word used by trainer Paul Nicholls to describe the demolition job his most prized asset doled out to his five rivals in this Grade 1 event, putting himself firmly on the trail of the £1 million Betfair bonus. Ruby Walsh, the winning rider, could barely contain his excitement.

There was a sparkle in his eyes and a mile-wide smile as he crossed the line. And that's not all. Potentially exceptional horses do

HAYDOCK, 18 November 2006		
Betfair Chase		3m
1 Kauto Star	11-10f	R Walsh
2 Beef Or Salmon	4-1	A McNamara
3 L'Ami	7-2	AP McCoy
6 ran 17l, 1l		

Kauto Star and Ruby Walsh during the Betfair Chase at Haydock, 18 November 2006

things to jockeys, provide a feel that is something special. And Walsh admitted that this was one of those occasions.

'For the first time for a long time, I had sweaty palms coming racing today,' Walsh revealed, explaining the anticipation he was experiencing. 'It doesn't happen often, but I knew that if he won, and won well, this horse would give me my first realistic chance of winning a Gold Cup.

'I couldn't have asked for any more. He was different class. He's jumped well, lobbed round and popped away. And when he jumped the last and opened up, he just annihilated them.'

Seemingly never out of third gear all the way round, Kauto Star got into a wonderful rhythm of jumping as Ollie Magern took the field along at a brisk pace. He was still on a tight rein as he moved into second place in the straight, and Walsh remained motionless as he took command going to the last. Shaken up, the gelding put daylight between himself and his toiling pursuers to post a 17-length triumph.

Nicholls said: 'We'd have got a bit of stick if he'd been beaten today,' referring to his decision to go into uncharted waters over this longer trip.

'Neither Ruby nor I had any real doubts that he'd stay three miles,' he confirmed. 'But it's all very well thinking and even saying that. He had to prove it on the track. And today he did.'

He added: 'I'd been trying to win a Champion Chase with a Gold Cup horse! I don't mind that. His jumping is so much better over this trip, and remember, he's still only six. We won't be thinking about Tingle Creek Chases from now on. It's Kempton next for the King George and then the Gold Cup.'

Not surprisingly, Ladbrokes cut Kauto Star to 6-4 for the King George, and now go 4-1 (from 10) for the Gold Cup, the same price as War Of Attrition. William Hill promoted him to 3-1 favourite for the Gold Cup, easing War Of Attrition to 7-2.

Michael Hourigan, trainer of runner-up Beef Or Salmon, was pleased with his nine-time Grade 1 winner, and feels the form is solid. 'We were beaten by a serious horse, a horse who just might go and win the Gold Cup,' he said.

He was so impressive at Haydock that Racing Post Ratings made Kauto Star the best staying chaser of the last decade and only 5lb inferior to the legendary Desert Orchid. In an echo of the sublime grey's versatility, Kauto Star was given a surprise entry in the Tingle Creek Chase and just two weeks after winning over three miles for the first time he showed his awesome ability over the minimum trip to claim back-to-back victories in the Sandown Park feature. Jon Lees reported:

SANDOWN, 2 December 2006		
William Hill Tingle Creek Chase	2m	
1 Kauto Star	4-9f	R Walsh
2 Voy Por Ustedes	4-1	R Thornton
3 Oneway	66-1	R Johnson
7 ran 7l, 7l		

Clive Smith still has the text message stored on his mobile. 'The Tingle Creek will come too soon. If he was nine or ten, we could risk it' came the reply from Paul Nicholls to the suggestion of another crack at the Grade 1 showpiece by Kauto Star.

By being prepared to change tack, the champion trainer displayed an open-mindedness for which everyone at Sandown was grateful yesterday after another stunning effort.

A fortnight after producing the best staying performance for ten years in the Betfair Lancashire Chase, Kauto Star went top of the 2m division too with a consummate dismissal of Voy Por Ustedes, last year's Arkle Trophy winner.

His second successive win in the William Hill Tingle Creek saw his Totesport Cheltenham Gold Cup odds tumble to as low as 9-4 favourite (from 3) with William Hill.

Despite the exchange of texts, Kauto Star was being readied for a tilt at the Stan James King George VI Chase without another race when Smith had a further chat with Nicholls on Monday.

'I'd left it at that, then I spoke to him last Monday about something else and said, 'by the way, we ought to consider the Tingle Creek',' Smith recalled. 'Paul rang me back five minutes later and said, 'I've just had a word with Ruby and he thinks it's a good idea'. Paul was a

Kauto Star and Ruby Walsh clear the final fence in the Tingle Creek at Sandown, 2 December 2006

Ruby Walsh, Clive Smith and
Paul Nicholls with the Tingle Creek
trophy

little blinkered, and then he thought, why not? He's said it all in the *Racing Post* – he couldn't find an excuse.'

In the race, Kauto Star had no difficulty laying up with the gallop and jumped to the front at the last of the railway fences, the exit of Dempsey at the first of them having cost Central House all chance.

There, Ruby Walsh took a pull to let Voy Por Ustedes back alongside but was firmly in control after the pond fence, despite clipping the top of the second-last.

Walsh said: 'We'd gone a good gallop and there was no point setting sail for home down there. He was travelling and I just wanted some company. Choc [Robert Thornton] came upsides and we've quickened across to the pond fence. I jumped it better and it was all over in two strides. I was thinking of the King George then.

'He's exceptional. He's one of those where all you have to do is steer with one leg either side. I've never ridden a horse like him. It's so easy for him. He jumps so well at two, two and a half, or three miles. He's special.'

Kauto Star is a top-priced 4-5 favourite with Boylesports for the Stan James King George VI Chase – the sponsors went 8-11 from 5-6 – after his third win of the season.

Nicholls said: 'We'll see whether he has any scratches on him, and if everything's all right he'll be there; if he's not right he won't be.

'He'd have looked silly in his box today. If I'd had half an excuse I wouldn't have run him, and when Clive sent me his text last week, you ask him what the reply was. In this game you've got to keep an open mind and, as the week's gone on, he's been so well.

'He's just got class. Ruby said at the start it was as if he'd told him it was a two-mile race, because he's immediately switched on and was jumping and travelling. You can switch him off, like we did at Haydock as well. He's not gone left or right either.

'This wasn't a gamble. He ran how he looked. In three weeks he might stand on a stone, but when they're fit and well you want to run them. He's been sparkling all week. The only one who's been feeling pressure is me.

'At Cheltenham, if we had a year of very deep ground I don't have to run in the Gold Cup; I could run in the Ryanair Chase or the Champion Chase. You don't have to have everything set in stone. You have to be versatile.'

Alastair Down was at Sandown to witness a most authoritative success in what was beginning to turn into a special season:

Kauto Star went into yesterday's Tingle Creek with 11st 7lb to carry, plus a weight of expectation beyond calculation.

Young horses brimful of promise are hardly two a penny, but what marks this one out is that he now fits the mould of the great all-rounders. Kauto Star is not, repeat not, as yet a Desert Orchid – that great grey edifice was eight hard seasons in the chiselling – but he can now be guided down any road from two to three miles plus and rare indeed are the sets of hooves who can meet that challenge at the highest level.

And, having turned the Tingle Creek into the most elementary of cakewalks, Kauto Star's status with the public will undergo a subtle but palpable sea-change. He began the afternoon the subject of admiration and a horse riding a wave of mounting excitement. By the end of the day he had confirmed himself good enough, potentially great enough, for us all to start worrying about him whenever he runs.

Opposite: Clifford Baker introduces his daughter Charlotte to Kauto Star

From now on thousands of others will join Ruby Walsh in riding him into every fence and Clive Smith, whom we have to thank for sowing the seed of this triumph in Paul Nicholls' mind, will find that, having been sole owner, he is now in a syndicate with more members than the AA and RAC combined.

Nicholls will have been under plenty of strain in recent days because, for all the sportsmanship of jump racing, the snipers are always out there waiting for their chance alongside the after-timers, told-you-so merchants and stiletto sliders.

But, as yesterday proved, we are fortunate that Kauto Star is owned and trained by men with – and I use the term in its most literal sense – the courage of their convictions.

Smith and Nicholls have long been convinced that they have something extraordinary on their hands and that is both a joy and a heavy responsibility. By coming to Sandown they sent out a clear message that, while they would never exploit this horse, they were not going to shirk any battles with him that they were convinced he could win.

In the end, the decision to run in the Tingle Creek was made by Kauto Star himself as he was clearly in such thumping good nick at home that there was every chance he would simply explode with sheer wellbeing if they didn't get his back down before King George day.

The race itself proved a formality waiting to be concluded. You don't often hear the expression 'hunting round' employed by a commentator in a top-class 2m chase, but that was Simon Holt's choice of words midrace and he was spot-on.

Walsh and Kauto Star made a shape through the race like a hawk among house sparrows, the inevitability of their superiority oozing from every pore, despite the fact that there was some quality opposition on hand.

If Kauto Star makes us work for his art it lies in that still uneradicated propensity to make the odd mistake. Ruby blamed himself for the error at the second-last and said the horse 'got him out of jail'.

After his Haydock win I had wondered whether the quicker pace of the King George might put pressure on his jumping. Kempton is a

trickier track than many realise and the jockeys on Kauto Star's rivals would be employing every trick in the book to force errors out of him. This is a game of cold blood and deadly earnest at the top level and the lads try everything within the rules and a few ruses outside them if they can get away with it. Remember Paul Carberry trying to poop the Best Mate party? Some thought it bad, but it was also brilliant.

But fears about the King George evaporated yesterday and the more urgent question about that race is just how many are going to have the bottle to turn up and oppose him. He is odds-on for Kempton and exerts an increasingly tight grip on the Gold Cup market. Were he being quoted for the Champion Chase he'd top that list as well.

As for measuring his quality, look no further than the observation from senior handicapper Phil Smith that, for the first time since the Anglo-Irish qualifications began in the late 90s, there is one horse top-rated at two, two and a half and three miles.

But the abiding impression was left by Kauto Star's demeanour in the winner's enclosure. A blind bat could have told you that he hadn't had a hard race, but he stood there looking as if he hadn't had a race at all. Ears pricked at the surrounding fuss and hubbub, he hadn't turned a hair. There was something almost unnatural about his air of ease and apparent lack of exertion. That is the mark of a good one, I suppose.

Greatness awaits Kauto Star and the racing public will wish him fair wind on the voyage to its realisation.

It was abundantly clear that racing's new star had caught the public's imagination, and in the run-up to the King George Nicholls insisted that 'three miles was made for Kauto Star'.

He gave the Boxing Day crowd a post-Christmas treat despite delivering everyone a right fright at the final fence in what was becoming a regular cover-your-eyes moment. Jon Lees reported:

A £1 million bonus is only one race and, critically, 22 fences away from the grasp of Kauto Star, but connections could be in for a roller-coaster ride for the riches after witnessing an eventful contest at Kempton yesterday.

KEMPTON, 26 December 2006		
Stan James King George VI Chase	3m	
1 Kauto Star	8-13f	R Walsh
2 Exotic Dancer	9-1	AP McCoy
3 Racing Demon	7-1	T Murphy
9 ran 8l, 1 ¾l		

Kauto Star crashes through the last fence before winning his first King George VI Chase at Kempton, 26 December 2006

Leaving hearts in mouths not once but twice during the climax to the Stan James King George VI Chase, Kauto Star nevertheless rode his luck and remains on course for the Totesport Cheltenham Gold Cup – and the Betfair Million bonus – in March.

He is a top-priced 2-1 (from 9-4) with Coral to lift the prize, yet in the course of recording an eight-length defeat of Exotic Dancer, with Racing Demon third, there emerged definite signs of an Achilles heel on the season's outstanding horse.

In front of a 21,000 near-full house, Kauto Star was fortunate to survive a howler at the fourth-last, and blundered through the final fence as well – errors that connections were keen to attribute to lack of concentration – yet he still won easily under Ruby Walsh.

'It was a hell of a performance, but you would just prefer it if he didn't make those mistakes,' said a relieved Walsh afterwards. 'Maybe it's lack of concentration, but heading into the back straight

Ruby Walsh and Kauto Star make it over the last fence before winning the 2006 King George

he was going in a length behind and coming out a length in front. He has an unbelievable jump in him.

'Why he does it, I don't know. We'll have to sit down and have a think and see how we can sort it out. Four out, I thought 'I'm lucky to be here', but then halfway round the bend I thought 'I'm still going to win'. When he missed the last I thought, 'Oh Jesus, don't get beat now'.'

Up until then, the race had been progressing without incident for Kauto Star. On the outer throughout, to accommodate his mount's tendency to jump to his left, Walsh found Kauto Star jumping with such exuberance that he was at pains to prevent him taking the lead too soon.

Kauto Star was given his head three out, the error at the fourth-last having barely checked his momentum, and after breasting the last, he was driven clear on the run-in.

Over three miles at Haydock, Walsh had ridden a waiting race on Kauto Star, but at Kempton the jockey said such tactics could not have been executed successfully.

'The first year I rode in the King George, John Francome told me you have to be up there turning in, upsides at the third-last,' said Walsh. 'It's a different track and a different race. You have to ride the race to suit the track. The Gold Cup is a different race, you can take

Paul Nicholls and Clive Smith wait for
Kauto Star in the winner's enclosure at
Kempton, with Anthony Bromley (right)

your time more. Haydock is a different track, but you can't drop in
around Kempton because you don't get into the race.'

Nicholls said: 'At Aintree he did exactly the same thing –
half-stepped at the last fence. Here, you have the big screen and the
crowd, and I think he's taken his eye off the ball a bit, but he's won
and that's all that matters.

'His best round of jumping was at Haydock, where we dropped
him out, crept and took our time with things. We couldn't do that
here because they were all going to go a good gallop round an easy
track, and we had to ride him a bit more positively.

'If he runs in the Gold Cup, we'll drop him in, take our time and
not arrive there too soon. Let's not go on about his jumping – he's
won well today.'

Owner Clive Smith had an air of calmness in the immediate
aftermath, but the palpitations he admitted to as he watched Kauto
Star add the second leg of the Betfair Million – having won the Betfair
Lancashire Chase at Haydock – could stand him in good stead for
Cheltenham.

'My heart was beating so much it nearly exploded. It's a great
relief to get through that,' he said. 'Part of his jumping wasn't great,
but he seemed to be able to plough his way through. He's obviously a
great horse in the making, as he's only six.'

Alastair Down was as taken by this performance as he had been at Sandown three weeks earlier:

So what manner of animal do we have in Kauto Star? A bewitchingly exceptional one who looks vulnerable to just one horse in training – himself. His supporters will insist he is not a bad jumper, but even the most purblind admirer cannot maintain he is a good jumper of fences. Two palpable howlers yesterday – four from home and again at the last – would have put paid to lesser horses, but he merely shrugged them off like a very classy middleweight taking one on the chin before resuming normal service and moving in for the kill.

It happened two out in the Tingle Creek, so we know it isn't stopping him, but the worrying common theme of these mistakes is that every time he makes one he is doing the well-nigh impossible – wrong-footing Ruby Walsh.

Ruby said afterwards: 'I don't know why he does it,' but what I suspect he really means is: 'I wish the hell I knew how he does it, and that the silly fellow would give me a bit of warning that he was about to.'

What was extraordinary about both Kauto Star's blunders was that they took place at the business end of a King George. These weren't out-in-the-country, early-stage errors in some cross-country amble at Towcester, they were in the very heat of Grade 1 action, when making such mistakes cost most horses the race. Yet they made no difference to the outcome.

All right, Kauto Star cannot be filed under 'most horses', but the worry is that either the tendency to clout one every now and again is eradicated, or he will eventually pay the price and fall again – with the Gold Cup's unique degree of difficulty a major concern.

It was interesting to my mind that Paul Nicholls asked Ruby down last Thursday to school him over 20 fences – ten of them ditches – in the loose school. Practice can indeed make perfect, but it also strikes me as tacit acknowledgement from the trainer that this chink in Kauto Star's armour has yet to be fully closed.

The answer to Ruby's question as to 'why he does it' might be that he is finding the whole process of racing so easy that his mind begins to wander to such topics as how bad the traffic is going to be on the way home to Ditcheat, like a top-class batsman who has knocked up a brilliant century without giving the ghost of a chance can suddenly stop concentrating for a second, waft airily at one outside the off stump, and be out needlessly for 106.

One thing for sure is that part of the bond the public is forging with Kauto Star is that, more than ever, they will have their hearts in their mouths every time one of those birch barriers looms into his path. It is never going be to dull or easy watching him, and we are all in for a refresher course on the meaning of the expression 'the edge of error'.

Two aspects of Kauto Star's performance should not be lost in the general obsession with the two errors he made yesterday. Ruby had loads of horse still under him late on because he noticeably lengthened on the run down to the last, and even after the momentum-sapping mistake there he proceeded to stay on strongly to the line.

Clifford Baker gives Kauto Star a workout at a picturesque Ditcheat

So, on a day that reminded us that Kempton is very much the spiritual home of the King George, the race fully lived up to its billing with the first four in the market looming up to do battle as it came to the boil in earnest. As for the Gold Cup, there will be bookies keen to get Kauto Star on the day, on the basis that mistakes in that neck-or-nothing event tend to exact high prices.

But to throw in two serious mis-reads such as Kauto Star did here and still win a King George unfussed is not the work of an everyday horse, and it makes him, potentially, even more remarkable.

There will be an awful lot riding on Kauto Star come Gold Cup day – and even more riding on the man riding him, with every fence a drama. Kauto Star and Ruby Walsh are a team of all the talents, and if the horse lets the jockey do the thinking, then they will give us a great day indeed.

Despite those mistakes in the King George, Nicholls was confident that going left-handed in the Gold Cup would not be a problem for Kauto Star.

In the Aon Chase at Newbury punters held their breath at the final fence again as Kauto survived another blunder, but he put himself in pole position for Cheltenham Gold Cup glory, as Jon Lees reported:

A nailbiting ordeal is promised at Cheltenham for all associated with Kauto Star, as they head to the Gold Cup knowing there is a potentially serious flaw in the favourite's challenge after another winning display yesterday was marred by an inexplicable last-fence blunder.

As a festival warm-up, Paul Nicholls had wanted a performance akin to those produced at Aintree and Haydock this season, but instead he endured a near rerun of Kempton at Christmas, when a pair of blunders almost cost Kauto Star victory in the King George VI Chase.

Yesterday, just when success in the Aon Chase seemed assured, he was nearly down when splitting the birch at the final fence, yet scrambled home by a neck from L'Ami after a furious sprint to the line, a result that saw his Gold Cup price ease slightly. He is now out to 7-4 with both William Hill and Totesport.

'We're coming to expect it now of him, but it's frustrating because he jumped brilliantly, foot-perfect, just stepped at the last,' said Nicholls. 'They've gone no gallop and he's run free all the way, but

Opposite: Kauto Star with Clifford Baker in his stable at Ditcheat

NEWBURY, 10 February 2007			
Aon Chase		3m	
1	Kauto Star	2-9f	R Walsh
2	L'Ami	6-1	AP McCoy
3	Royal Auclair	40-1	L Heard
6 ran nk, 14l			

Opposite: Kauto Star ploughs through the final fence in the Aon Chase at Newbury, 10 February 2007

one positive is that Ruby says he'll definitely get the trip in the Gold Cup because he keeps on galloping.

'We've got to live with it. No amount of schooling will make any difference and he should know better, but bear in mind he's three-parts fit and will come on an awful lot for that. It's in the lap of the gods. He did reorganise himself and ran on well for Ruby, but I just wish he didn't do what he did at the last.

'It's almost like he's got into the habit that he's going to hurdle the last fence. He tries to bank them and it's the second time he's done it. We have a month to really tune him up and we'll go on from there.'

Jockey Ruby Walsh was ordered to drop anchor on Kauto Star and not produce him before the last, but the pace was so sedate that Kauto Star was still on the bridle when joining the lead two out. From there the race was on and, with L'Ami challenging, Kauto Star clattered through the last fence yet stayed upright, an error that Walsh did well to survive, and was still able to muster the speed to gain the spoils at the end of a race owner Clive Smith admitted had been 'agony to watch'.

A mystified Walsh said: 'He just stays standing. He ran at the fence. He ran very keen all the way and was probably getting a bit empty. He seems to put down and lands galloping, I don't know why. It felt like he banked it. He's making a bit of a habit of it.'

The experience will provide some food for thought over the coming weeks, since the tactics here were expected to iron out the achilles heel that had been in evidence at Kempton and now Newbury.

Nicholls added: 'Ruby might want now to think about how he's going to ride him in the Gold Cup, because he might want to do it differently at Cheltenham.

'I said, "Whatever you do I don't want you in front before the last." I wanted him covered up to get the trip, a little bit like he was at Haydock. His best round of jumping was in the Tingle Creek, when they were really attacking their fences. A race like this doesn't really suit him.'

After making it five out of five for the season at Newbury, Kauto Star would face the ultimate test in the Gold Cup, according to Alastair Down:

On as classy an afternoon as you could stumble over outside of Cheltenham and Aintree, Kauto Star showed once again that he is a half-brother to a Polo – he's mint, but there's a hole in him.

This time Kauto Star's twig-shredder at the last couldn't be put down to dossing or losing his concentration, as he was having to battle in earnest against L'Ami when once again giving his supporters palpitations when it looked all over bar the shouting.

Ruby Walsh had to haul him back on to an even keel to get him to run right in order to pick up the inner rail again and, to the horse's credit, he pulled out plenty to seal the issue.

In his column in yesterday's *Post*, Paul Nicholls wrote: 'If there's anyone who is worried about his jumping, my advice to them is to go and watch the videos of him winning at Aintree and Haydock. He was simply brilliant, never making the semblance of a mistake.'

The trite answer to that is that anyone who is not worried about his jumping only needs to watch the Tingle Creek, King George and the final fence here to convince themselves that Kauto Star's capacity to make a serious error unbidden and unheralded is what stands between him and Gold Cup victory.

Interviewed on television, Nicholls' face said it all – a mixture of concern, frustration and bafflement. It isn't that Kauto Star is in any way an intrinsically bad jumper, but lurking inside him is this accident waiting to happen. Lesser men than Ruby would have parted company with him already this season.

If he puts in a clear round at Cheltenham, the book says they won't see which way he goes, but the rough-house of the Gold Cup will be the greatest test he has faced to date and every piece of gamesmanship made by God or the devil will be employed against him.

There is nothing Nicholls can do but sit and suffer. If Kauto Star's technique looked palpably ropey, you could send him to Yogi Breisner to stop him making a boo-boo, but he does the basics well and, until the last, jumped almost flawlessly.

The problem now is that Ruby, for all his cool-headedness, will be going round Cheltenham with a fair chunk of his mind on the qui vive for the sky falling in. Mind you, with plenty of pace on, it is more than likely he will be able to drop Kauto Star in and click into the all-essential rhythm that will get him round the ups and downs of God's own racecourse without mishap.

One thing's for sure – there will be 60,000 hearts in mouths every time Kauto Star approaches a fence and the fate of the favourite takes flight.

Kauto Star was red-hot favourite for the 2007 Gold Cup and Paul Nicholls was a calm of oasis in the build-up to this date with destiny. 'Lots of people are getting worked up about his jumping in the Gold Cup, but we're not worrying too much and it's not something I'm losing any sleep over,' he said.

While his trainer exuded confidence, Clive Smith was plain excited – and not just because he had backed Kauto Star on Betfair at 140 – as Peter Thomas reported.

Clive Smith has vivid memories of his first Cheltenham Gold Cup and they come flooding back whenever he thinks of his, and Kauto Star's, next day in the spotlight.

'I remember it clearly,' he says. 'It was 1974 and I was hanging off the railings to see Pendil. I'd backed him at odds-on, which wasn't very clever in a race like the Gold Cup, I suppose, but he was such a great horse, and he was going well until he was brought down at the third-last. I was reminded of that thinking about Kauto Star.'

Many might take this to mean that Smith has recurring nightmares of his chasing superstar, currently 15-8 in the betting for the big one, being turned over in front of an audience of his most ardent admirers, losing the race that destiny seemed to have prepared him for.

'No, it's not that at all,' he says. 'It's just the excitement of the day and the atmosphere and how great it will be going there this year. And I haven't had to bet at odds-on this time – I've backed him at 140 on Betfair, not to very much, but enough to buy a few bottles of champagne!

'I know how tough the festival can be, though. My horse Hawthorn Blaze had won four out of four when we aimed him there in 1993, and Peter Scudamore wrote in the Monday's paper that he was his best bet of the week in the Arkle.

Opposite: Kauto Star goes through
the final fence again before claiming
a first Cheltenham Gold Cup success,
16 March 2007

'I headed down there, arrived at the hotel on Monday evening, then got a phone call from Martin Pipe to say he couldn't run. And we missed the same race with Kauto Star two years ago after he came down at Exeter. It's made me more philosophical, though, rather than more nervous as we head towards the Gold Cup. The excitement is there, but you know these things can happen.'

If Kauto Star is to lose the Gold Cup, the popular view is that he will lose it by attempting to flatten one or both of the last two fences, as he has done at more than one track this season. But Smith remains resolutely optimistic that this wrinkle will be ironed out before the big day. And he also thinks we have yet to see the best of the seven-year-old.

He says: 'The feeling in the yard is that he can get even better – he's still a young horse. He's made a new life for me and if he stays sound, we could be talking like this in two or three years' time.'

On the morning of the Gold Cup Nicholls said it was time for Kauto Star to prove his doubters wrong and win the Cheltenham Gold Cup. As Jon Lees reported, he did just that:

The windfall ranks as the biggest in jumps racing history, but it was a reputation that was the more prized commodity on the day Kauto Star claimed the Cheltenham Gold Cup yesterday.

The massive sum of £1.24 million was riding on Kauto Star landing Gold Cup glory, yet his credibility was also at stake.

Despite a perfect campaign, with victories in defining races like the Tingle Creek Trophy and King George VI Chase that established him as the most outstanding chaser for a generation, the jury was still out.

Jumping mistakes in his races had exposed a weakness and opinion was split until yesterday, when Kauto Star rose to the challenge and healed the divisions with the victory on which he will properly be judged.

At the track where he had made an ignominious third-fence exit from the Queen Mother Champion Chase a year earlier, he produced the ideal riposte under Ruby Walsh to defeat Exotic Dancer.

His victory march yet again included a last-fence scare, but it failed to check his momentum as he strolled towards a famous and

CHELTENHAM, 16 March 2007		
Totesport Cheltenham Gold Cup Chase	3m2½f	
1 Kauto Star	5-4f	R Walsh
2 Exotic Dancer	9-2	AP McCoy
3 Turpin Green	40-1	T Dobbin
18 ran 2½l, 2½l		

lucrative win that netted owner Clive Smith and the Paul Nicholls stable the Betfair bonus, a share of £1m for completing wins in the Betfair Chase, King George and Gold Cup.

It ended a challenging period for jump racing's champion trainer, to whom the questioning of Kauto Star's ability seemed less healthy debate and more character assassination.

'I cannot tell you how nerve-racking the last four weeks have been,' he said.

'I've never heard so much rubbish talked about him. He's won six on the trot and in the Tingle Creek he beat the Champion Chase winner, yet there were all these doubters. He is a brilliant horse.

'I knew at Newbury he was half fit. I'd done nothing with him since Kempton. I didn't need to. Today was the day I wanted him at his best. I worked him hard since then and got him fit and relaxed. He was brilliant today and he had the right man on board.

'I'm sure going to the last he was just going so well he loses concentration a fraction. He is awesome, a very, very good horse. You always think he is going to make a mistake but he never looks like falling. What is on his mind I don't know, but he is obviously not tired.

'This win is not just good for me, it's good for racing. It needs a superstar and he has proved himself here. I've just been amazed how much he has been knocked, but we always believed in him and being positive has helped.'

A tense Nicholls had broken away from the main throng to watch the race unfold alone on a TV screen at a Tote outlet. Kauto Star, heavily supported into 5-4, gave him little cause for concern.

Anchored on the rail from the outset by Ruby Walsh, he was a bit low over one fence on the first circuit but jumped cleanly everywhere else.

With Idle Talk losing his jockey early, the greater concern was the congestion that began to build up second time round with a loose horse among them.

As a result, Walsh was forced to switch to the outside approaching the third-last and, clear of traffic, Kauto Star surged to the front at the second-last and, although brushing through the last, ran on powerfully to score by two and a half lengths.

It was Exotic Dancer, who had sat out the back for much of the way, who picked his way through the field to take second from Turpin Green in third and Monkerhostin back in fourth – the last two also purchases made by bloodstock agent Anthony Bromley, who had bought Kauto Star for €400,000.

Bromley's client Smith can celebrate a profitable transaction and in victory fulfilled a long-standing ambition.

'I'm so delighted,' he said. 'I can't tell you how thrilled I am. After two out I thought he would definitely win. I think he just teased us at the last and then he was clear.

'I'm totally excited. I've had horses since 1987, so for 20 years I had hoped that one day I might win this. I'm pleased as punch. The money will go but the Gold Cup will always be with me.

'Paul Nicholls has been spot-on all the way through and I would like to pay due credit to Paul and his magnificent team.'

Kauto Star will return next term with another Gold Cup win as his goal, although the festival has seen another rival to his crown emerge in Royal & SunAlliance Chase winner Denman. Neither horse, 2-1 favourite and 4-1 second favourite for next year's Gold Cup with bookmakers Coral, will run again this term.

Nicholls said: 'This year he has run six races and won six. Next year there is only going to be one target and that is the Cheltenham Gold Cup, so I guess we will build our season round that, but I would love to win the Tingle Creek with him for the third time.

'He and Denman will meet one day but it certainly won't be at Kempton. That course wouldn't suit Denman, who will probably go to Leopardstown, leaving Kauto Star for the King George, but let us enjoy the moment and worry about that problem when it arises.'

Alastair Down gave his assessment of the towering performance he had witnessed:

Winning a Gold Cup doesn't confer greatness of itself, but no staying chaser holds his place in history unless he succeeds in the main event at Cheltenham and Kauto Star is on his way to God knows where in jumping's scheme of things after his triumph yesterday.

In the run-up to the race Paul Nicholls, irked by the perfectly reasonable observations of all and sundry that his pride and joy can

Right: Ruby Walsh celebrates winning
his first Cheltenham Gold Cup

hit the odd fence, was heard saying: 'He's won five in row, what more do they want?' Well the answer to that question is that they – the racing public – wanted him to win the Gold Cup.

The passion may not have been as white-hot as that of Nicholls, Ruby Walsh, Clive Smith and all the team at Ditcheat but, in our own way, we wanted Kauto Star to prove himself beyond any doubt because we, too, need our fleeting brush with brilliance, even if it is at one remove.

It was an extraordinary Gold Cup in that, as they came round the home turn, there was a whole pack of horses still apparently in contention.

But, in reality, only Kauto Star and Exotic Dancer were travelling like horses with something to add to the argument, and from when the favourite jumped into the lead two out there could be only one conclusion, unless the sky fell in at the last.

At the risk of aggravating Nicholls in the hour of his vindication, if he didn't have a bother on him as Ruby powered down to the final fence, the rest of us were all too aware that, in the past, this has been the moment Kauto Star occasionally indulged in his party trick of whacking one.

And like an old trouper going through a familiar routine, he did it again just to keep his fans on their toes, though there wasn't even a fleeting moment when he looked like coming to grief.

Nicholls is bang right when he insists his horse is essentially a good jumper but the horse's critics – many of whom are also fans – are not talking through the top of their heads when they point out that he not only makes mistakes but will soon be able to patent his own very distinctive Kauto-esque high-speed brush through the fence three-quarters of the way up.

But the bull point here is that he doesn't fall and, of course, can't get rid of Ruby who wouldn't unseat if he was perched atop of Vesuvius on an eruption day.

There will be the usual folk in need of psychiatric help and a seamstress to sew a new patch on their anoraks who say this was a bad Gold Cup, citing the presence of Turpin Green in third and Monkerthostin fourth as evidence for the prosecution.

Bilge. In a very muddling Gold Cup, with dear old Beef Or Salmon among the leaders for more than a circuit, the two best chasers of the season emerged to make total sense of the race by finishing first and second.

So we have a chasing star of real substance and one who will have vastly cemented his place in racing's popular affections.

It helps both in the saddle and out of it that he is ridden by Ruby Walsh, who is such a transparently decent bloke as well as being a jockey with a thousand and one different ways of riding a racehorse.

Kauto Star parades in Ditcheat the
day after his Gold Cup victory

I have never seen anyone with a wider range of abilities in the saddle and the public trust him utterly.

Kauto Star and Denman, along with Nicholls' other festival winners, returned home to a hero's reception in Ditcheat. Lee Mottershead was among the happy throng:

Britain's wealthiest racehorse has quickly adapted to his new status. Walk into Kauto Star's box, where the straw bedding has been replaced with the finest Axminster, and the scent of expensive cigar smoke hangs in the air. Sky Plus is being installed for the millionaire gelding next week, and there's even talk of him joining forces with Denman to put in a bid for the *Racing Post*. Who says money doesn't change horses?

This is the day after the day before. It is Ditcheat's day. At 12.30pm, Kauto Star and Denman, one the Gold Cup hero, one the pretender to his throne, join Paul Nicholls' other Cheltenham Festival winners Taranis and Andreas for a parade down the road that links one end of Ditcheat to the other.

Fifteen minutes earlier, Ditcheat looks not so much like a sleepy Somerset village, more a comatosed one. Then, the cottages empty and at least 200 locals converge outside the Manor House Inn, lining the road on both sides to give the fabulous four a roar only marginally less thunderous than the one that greeted the start of the Gold Cup.

'We didn't even advertise that this was taking place,' says Nicholls, clearly taken aback by the reception the horses and his team have received.

'The village is so much a part of it,' explains Marianne Barber, wife of Nicholls' landlord Paul Barber. 'There are even people here who don't live in Ditcheat – the yard has such a following.'

One of those people is Annabel Smith. Happy to be one of Nicholls' smaller owners, she has come 12 miles from her home in Green Ore just to see the star chasers parade and share in the feeling of communal joy.

'I know all the horses and love them,' she says. 'Sonja [Warburton], who looks after Kauto Star, is like a second daughter to me.

'I came down when See More Business was paraded after he won his Gold Cup, and this is like deja vu. They didn't have to parade them again, but it's so lovely that they have. It's very emotional.'

Not only is Kauto Star good enough, he is the best, the real deal, the true champion whose coronation led to celebrations of the very highest and most tiddly order. Not surprisingly, not everyone is looking at their best, particularly assistant trainer Dan Skelton, who had to be driven to Uttoxeter by his girlfriend after partaking of too many shandies. The exception appears to be Nicholls' partner Georgie Browne, although she admits to artificial assistance. 'The make-up was trowelled on this morning,' she says. 'Don't ask me for details about when I got to bed, though. I've absolutely no idea.'

Clifford Baker, head groom to Nicholls and the man who gets to ride Kauto Star every morning, has. 'I got back in at 2.35am, turned on the telly and the Gold Cup happened to be showing on Racing UK. I've watched it half a dozen times now and never get tired of it. This is my third Gold Cup, because I was with Charter Party before See More Business, but I think this fellow is a little better – he's got that little bit extra.'

He also appears to know that he is special. Before the parade, he stands to attention for a multitude of photographers, handsome head

Previous spread: Kauto Star (right) and stablemate Denman eye each other up at Manor Farm Stables

Below: Kauto Star says hello to his groom Sonja Warburton

poked out of box, posing when requested. The horse who regularly nods goodbye to visitors driving out of the yard has made his owner Clive Smith an even richer man, but Betfair's £1 million bonus is not what Friday was about. It was about the Gold Cup, the tiny trophy that Nicholls' youngest daughter Olivia is keen to stick her head inside for closer study.

'If we had been second at Kempton and the £1m had gone, I would still have been as ecstatic standing here with the Gold Cup,' says Smith.

'Today is wonderful. The village is enjoying being a part of it because the village is a part of it. I've only just recovered from last night, though. Thirty-four of us had dinner, lots of champagne and finished off with armagnac. I went to bed at 2am but got up at 5am because I couldn't wait to get the papers.'

Kauto Star parades in front of the spectators on the final day of the season at Sandown Park on 28 April 2007

They will have made happy reading, not least for the triumphant trainer. 'Out on his feet' at 1.30am, he re-watched the Gold Cup before going to bed and then once more on getting up at 5.30am.

'It still hasn't sunk in yet,' he admits. 'My feet haven't touched the ground, and I keep going round with a smile on my face. Days like these mean so much, they are what it's all about. I'd honestly rather win the big races than the trainers' championship – it's more likely you get remembered for winning two Gold Cups than two championships.'

Down at the Manor, Team Ditcheat and the locals continue to celebrate. While they do so, at 2.30pm a small, white car drives into Nicholls' empty yard. Out of the car gets a little old man. He walks straight to Kauto Star's box and strokes the head of the Gold Cup victor. He then walks back to his car, gets in and drives off.

Kauto nods goodbye.

The superstar of the jumps season paraded at Sandown in April sunshine on the last day of the campaign to round off an extraordinary year.

A career in Britain that had started with so much promise just two and a half years earlier had now delivered so much. It was time for Kauto to have a summer's rest before trying to emulate Best Mate and retain his Gold Cup crown.

4

The rivals

*AFTER A STELLAR 2006-07 it was back to business in the autumn,
and Nicholls reported Kauto Star to be in super condition in October:
'He looks fab and is going nicely at home, working every bit as well as
at this corresponding stage last year. It was awesome what he achieved
last season – frustrating, I admit, that he made those silly mistakes, but
Ruby knows a lot more about him now, and so do I, and there are a few
things we can do to help in that respect.'*

*Kauto faced a huge task on his seasonal debut in the Old Roan Chase
at Aintree as he was forced to concede lumps of weight to the likes of
Exotic Dancer, Monet's Garden and Ashley Brook.*

*Although he was denied by Nicky Richards's outstanding grey, there
was no honour lost in defeat, as Colin Russell reported:*

Beaten but by no means bowed.

The unbeaten run of the 2007 Gold Cup hero Kauto Star came to
an end yesterday when he finished an honourable second to the grey
Monet's Garden, who galloped his way to a memorable win.

Giving a stone to a horse who, just seven months earlier, had won
the Grade 1 John Smith's Melling Chase at the track, proved a bridge
too far for last season's phenomenon.

Kauto Star had come off the bridle soon after halfway but never
stopped battling, in the end succumbing by a length and a half.

Despite the defeat, he remains a best-priced 2-1 with Betfred to
take Cheltenham gold again, and 6-4 favourite for the Stan James
King George VI Chase at Kempton on Boxing Day.

Nicholls was not at all disappointed with Kauto Star: 'Never mind
not staying, he needs three miles these days. Ruby said he was
running lazily and needs further than this.

'We always said the winner would be a big danger, we had to give
him a lot of weight and he's a specialist two-and-a-half-miler.

'My horse will now go to Haydock for the Betfair Chase, as
planned. This will have put him right for that.'

*There was one change for Haydock, though, as Sam Thomas was called
up to partner Kauto after Ruby Walsh dislocated his shoulder in a fall*

AINTREE, 28 October 2007		
Bonusprint.com Old Roan Chase (Limited handicap)		2m4f
1 Monet's Garden	9-4	T Dobbin
2 Kauto Star	11-10f	R Walsh
3 Exotic Dancer	9-2	AP McCoy
4 ran 1½l, 20l		

at Cheltenham's Paddy Power meeting. Everyone was happy with that decision, but Clive Smith expressed fears about whether we had seen the best of Kauto Star, as he told Peter Thomas in late November:

Clive Smith, the owner of Kauto Star, admitted yesterday to fears that his Cheltenham Gold Cup hero may have reached the peak of his achievements, but vowed to press on in his bid to challenge the supremacy of the stars of yesteryear.

He said: 'They say sometimes that these French horses don't train on and his last piece of form can be interpreted in different ways, both positive and negative.

'It may be that six races in a season have left their mark, but we do know that he can stay all the distances and Paul says he is in great form.

'Now we just want to see him prove himself again. It would be lovely to hear him mentioned in the same breath as Arkle, and I know people are talking about it and saying he's not there yet, but it would be good for racing if he were to win on Saturday [at Haydock] and begin to show how good he is.'

Smith was also quick to dismiss claims that he was concerned about Sam Thomas standing in for the injured Ruby Walsh at the weekend.

He said: 'Victory at the weekend would be great for Sam and I have every confidence in him. Paul thinks he's the man for the job and I'm happy with that. Now he has to show the bottle on the day and make the right decisions at the right time.

'He's a great substitute for Ruby.'

Kauto silenced any doubters with a second successive Betfair Chase victory, as Tom O'Ryan reported:

He's back. But, as Paul Nicholls so succinctly put it: 'Has he ever been away?'

Kauto Star, beaten at Aintree four weeks ago, put himself firmly back in the spotlight that he hogged exclusively last season with a brave and thrilling win in the Betfair Chase as he got the better of old adversary Exotic Dancer by half a length.

HAYDOCK, 24 November 2007			
Betfair Chase		3m	
1	Kauto Star	4-5f	S Thomas
2	Exotic Dancer	8-1	B Geraghty
3	Beef Or Salmon	28-1	D O'Regan
7 ran ½l, 18l			

The pair finished in a different parish to third-placed Beef Or Salmon after treating a bumper crowd to the sort of climax that raises neck hairs and quickens pulses.

Victory put Kauto Star on the first rung of the ladder to the Betfair Million, which he scooped last season after following his win in this race with victories in the King George VI Chase and the Cheltenham Gold Cup. Ladbrokes go 3-1 about a repeat.

The win was greeted with whoops of delight from his legions of fans, who dutifully cheered him back to the winner's enclosure under Sam Thomas, who proved an effective deputy for the injured Ruby Walsh.

The 23-year-old Welshman, having given the highest-profile jumper in training a wonderful ride – 'I just rode like a normal race' – was praised by Nicholls for his initiative in changing tactics when Paddy Brennan set off like a scalded cat on Ollie Magern before giving way to the winner, who produced a mighty leap to take the lead five from home.

'We discussed beforehand everything that might happen, and all credit to Sam for using his head. We were going to drop in and creep into the race but, the way it went, he had to ride him handier. He's been left in front sooner than ideal, but he battled when it mattered,' said Nicholls before reflecting on Kauto Star's Old Roan Chase defeat on his comeback.

'I said all along that Aintree was a stepping-stone to here, which is the one that mattered; this, and the Gold Cup, with the King George along the way.

'He was beaten by a very good horse at Aintree in Monet's Garden, trying to give him a stone. We're back where we belong again now. But were we ever away? He's still the one they've all got to beat in the Gold Cup.'

The Tingle Creek was ruled out by Nicholls in early December as all thoughts were concentrated on a second King George VI Chase victory on Boxing Day.

In early December, Kauto Star was crowned Horse of the Year – the first jumps horse to win the award for nine years – as Andrew Scutts reported:

Kauto Star may have been denied the chance to add another Tingle Creek to his list of achievements, but his cv was nonetheless looking

Opposite: Kauto Star and Sam Thomas jumping their way to Betfair Chase success at Haydock, 24 November 2007

even more impressive last night when he was crowned ROA/Racing Post Horse of the Year.

The Gold Cup hero became the first jumper to win the award since One Man in 1998 and he did so by polling more than three-quarters of the votes.

Racehorse Owners' Association members, of which there are 7,200, and readers of the *Racing Post* elected to honour Clive Smith's chaser in their droves, with his victories in last season's Betfair Chase, King George and Gold Cup, capturing the imagination.

Christmas was crucial for the Nicholls team, as Kauto had pleased his trainer in the run-up to the King George, while stablemate Denman was due to run in the Lexus Chase a month after he had put up a breathtaking performance to win the Hennessy Gold Cup at Newbury.

At Kempton the reigning Gold Cup winner strengthened his hold on the King George crown when he trounced Our Vic and Exotic Dancer. Jon Lees reported:

Many must-have gifts did not make it under the Christmas tree this year as demand in the high street outstripped supply, but at least one seasonal wish was fulfilled when Kauto Star delivered his most complete performance yesterday.

With his quality under scrutiny due to his first-time-out Aintree defeat and the emergence of stablemate Denman, the champion responded in the most convincing fashion, producing a faultless display to clinch a second Stan James King George VI Chase.

Even the final-fence blunder, such a worrying feature of his racing style on his way to a first Cheltenham Gold Cup triumph last season, had vanished from his repertoire, as Kauto Star dismissed Our Vic and long-standing rival Exotic Dancer by 11 lengths and a length and a quarter.

Temporarily dethroned as Gold Cup favourite after the Hennessy victory of Denman, Kauto Star was cut to as low as evens favourite (from 7-4) by William Hill, but was last night generally available at 6-4 to retain his crown in March.

Denman, who runs in Ireland's Lexus Chase tomorrow, remains 2-1 with Gold Cup sponsor Totesport.

KEMPTON, 26 December 2007

Stan James King George VI Chase 3m

1	Kauto Star	4-6f	R Walsh
2	Our Vic	12-1	T Murphy
3	Exotic Dancer	9-2	AP McCoy

7 ran 11l, 1¼l

Kauto Star and Ruby Walsh are the focus of attention before the King George VI Chase at Kempton, 26 December 2007

Kauto Star helped Kempton draw its biggest Boxing Day attendance for six years and he did not disappoint the 25,000-plus crowd, becoming the 12th horse to win the King George more than once and the eighth to do so in consecutive years.

Kempton is the track at which trainer Paul Nicholls believes Kauto Star is most vulnerable but, under Ruby Walsh, back in the saddle after a five-week absence, he was never under threat and when they moved to the front at the fourth-last, the prize was clinched.

Nicholls said: 'He's going to take some beating, isn't he? I told Ruby to be positive. Last year the mistake down the back was as much due to Ruby not wanting to hit the front too soon, but if he used his staying power they would never get by him.

'To me that was as good a performance as anything he's done before. He looks as good as he's ever looked. I was happy enough with him at Aintree, but I did think he raced a bit lazily. He's sharp now and is still the one they all have to beat.

'Denman is still stepping up the ladder, but on what we've seen he has got to keep progressing.'

Nicholls had been confident in Kauto Star, but admitted unease at having endured a leaner spell lately, with only four winners from 38 runners.

With Nicholls keen to give Kauto Star a run before the Gold Cup, he will depart from last year's programme, with the Commercial First Chase at Ascot on February 16 the first preference, while Denman will head for the Aon Chase at Newbury, won by Kauto Star last season.

Kauto Star and Ruby Walsh deliver a faultless performance

Back in the winner's enclosure for the first time in 40 days, Walsh said: 'It was all over when he jumped to the front at the fourth-last.

'As you could see, the way he jumped left in the straight, he's a better horse going in the other direction, so imagine if that was at Cheltenham and he didn't lose ground at his fences by going out to the left.'

Should Denman match Kauto Star with victory in Ireland tomorrow, the stage will be set for a showdown at Cheltenham, a clash Kauto Star's owner Clive Smith would look forward to.

'I don't mind,' said Smith. 'Let's have a race. I thought this was a real race with Exotic Dancer, but he left him behind. Denman has won a Grade 1 and we've won several. I think we're a bit ahead of him at the moment.'

Kauto Star was back in the ascendancy, and as Alastair Down reported from Kempton, his critics had nowhere to hide:

It was the day the carping stopped. Even the most mean-spirited critics among the jockeys in the stands were silenced as Kauto Star racked up his second King George, steaming home to win with all the world in hand and landing a heavy-duty thwack in the faces of those who have had the temerity to doubt him.

This was definitive stuff, the dream of the steeplechaser rampant as he jumped and galloped them groggy. A day after celebrating the virgin birth, Kauto Star was the immaculate conception.

And the most telling summation of what we saw came from AP McCoy who, with a mixture of admiration and head-shaking resignation, said: 'It is a bit depressing when you hear a jockey going "Whoa!" when running to the fourth-last in a King George.'

Depressing for McCoy, but astonishing and pulsating for nearly every other man jack at a heaving Kempton, because Kauto Star has never done his job better than he did here.

There was no semblance of a mistake and, although he has proven himself a thorough stayer, there is so much more to him than that dour description implies.

When you watch Kauto Star in full cry, however dark or gloomy the day, the twin gleams of class and speed keep glinting through like buried treasure promising further riches to come.

A beaming Ruby Walsh with Kauto Star in the winner's enclosure at Kempton

This fellow, remember, was the first horse in the modern age of official ratings to head the list at two, two and a half and three miles. As all-rounders go he is Botham in a bridle.

Fresh tactics on Exotic Dancer availed connections of nothing and with the score now five-nil to Kauto Star, there is little Jonjo O'Neill will be able to do about it, short of investing in a grenade launcher.

This was Kauto Star's most complete performance to date and handicapper Phil Smith confirmed he will edge him up another pound to the sort of rating that only the great ones can lay claim.

It is just a month since Denman set the jumps world on its ear with a Hennessy win that forced him up the Gold Cup market to equal favouritism.

But Kauto Star wrested back favouritism here and he is the one with the performances in the book, whereas Denman remains a rising force with points still to prove.

That the pair of them stick their noses out to sniff the air from adjacent boxes in the same stable is certainly without parallel since Arkle and Flyingbolt shared their lair at Greenogue.

Sporting precedents are hard to find. Perhaps Coe and Ovett wearing the Great Britain vest in their prime because, like those great middle-distance men, these two horses may indeed share a dressing room but they do not do so as team-mates. Rather, opponents out for individual glory.

And while you could envisage Kauto Star humping top weight to victory in the Hennessy, it is harder to imagine Denman winning a King George in the manner of his stablemate yesterday.

What we all need is for the pair to stay fit and well through to Cheltenham because we will never have a better opportunity to sell this sport than by pushing the showdown between them.

Daffy marketing schemes for racing are ten a penny, but this is a simple head-to-head clash that can be easily understood by the public and ratcheted up all the way through to March.

Comparing the two horses will be the sport of every racing pub and club for the next two and a half months, but it is the prospect of their meeting in March that is riveting.

Just think of the tension over the last half hour of the build-up as the time comes to put away the guns and swords and go fist to fist.

Characterising horses of this calibre is usually thankless or pointless. Kauto Star being the more brilliant may prove the more brittle. Denman has about him the durability of a miner's pick, but he could find Kauto Star's speed renders him too hard a rock to crack.

And so at Christmas, 'the season to be jolly', we have a season about which we can be jolly for months to come as we relish the sort of promoter's dream that every match-maker in boxing would give a limb for – the classic confrontation between the complete artist and the scrapper with talent.

If Kauto Star and Denman make it to Cheltenham on Gold Cup day you can stop the clock there and then.

Previous spread: Kauto Star (left)

April onwards can go hang, because it will already have been a very happy and remarkable new year.

All eyes turned to Leopardstown to see how Denman would fare in the Lexus Chase and Kauto's next-door neighbour did not disappoint, with a four-length victory over Mossbank.

It raised the question of who Walsh would ride at Cheltenham, but the Irishman wasn't pushed into making a decision.

'March is still far away and that is a decision for another day. They are two very good horses and it has been a great few days for me, winning two major races on them,' he said.

'Denman was very impressive today. He had to do it the hard way and showed that he can do the job regardless of the gallop. He quickened up when I asked him and was always doing enough. He wore out the others.'

After weeks of mounting anticipation the Irishman chose to retain his partnership with the Gold Cup winner, with Sam Thomas booked for Denman.

Walsh described the decision over which of the exciting chasers to ride as huge, but added: 'At the end of the day, how do you get off a Gold Cup winner?'

With the riding arrangements sorted it was time to get back to the racing, and a week after Denman put up a cracking performance in the Aon Chase at Newbury it was time for Kauto to respond in the Commercial First Ascot Chase.

Nicholls said it would take something special to beat Kauto. Although he won, he was found to be lame after the race, as Ben Newton and Jon Lees reported:

Kauto Star's bid for a second Cheltenham Gold Cup success was the subject of an injury scare last night after he was found to be lame behind following an impressive victory at Ascot.

However, trainer Paul Nicholls was not ruling his brilliant chaser out of the Gold Cup and will know more after Clive Smith's superstar is examined again by his vet Buffy Shirley-Beavan this morning.

Kauto Star had hardened as favourite for the Gold Cup following his eight-length defeat of Monet's Garden in the Commercial First Ascot Chase and had gone odds-on at 1.98 on Betfair.

ASCOT, 16 February 2008		
Commercial First Ascot Chase	2m5½f	
1 Kauto Star	4-11f	R Walsh
2 Monet's Garden	6-1	T Dobbin
3 Racing Demon	15-2	P Moloney
9 ran 8l, nk		

However, just after 6pm last night the eight-year-old was the subject of a sudden drift on the betting exchange, touching 4.7 – over 7-2 – with stablemate Denman taking over as market leader.

Nicholls said last night: 'Kauto Star was absolutely fine after the race. Donna [Blake, travelling head groom] gave him a pick of grass and he was absolutely fine, but when he went to be loaded on to the lorry it was noticed that he was lame behind.

'He has been x-rayed and there is no fracture. He will be examined by our vet at 8 o'clock tomorrow morning and then another statement will be made.'

Last night many of the major bookmakers had suspended betting on the race.

Kauto Star and Ruby Walsh during the Ascot Chase before his injury scare, 16 February 2008

Kauto Star and Ruby Walsh at Ascot:
poetry in motion

Nicholls had initially thought the injury was a sprained fetlock.
He later reported that the senior vet at Ascot, Sven Kold, had advised him that it was quite possible that there was an infection brewing in a foot, in which case a recovery could be much quicker.

Earlier in the day it had seemed that only an act of God would prevent Nicholls winning the Totesport-sponsored Gold Cup in 26 days' time.

The question racing had so badly wanted answering was with which of his two stars he would do it, and while Denman continues on the ascent, Kauto Star had shown that the final climb to chasing's summit would be extremely challenging with an emphatic triumph.

Set a more competitive test than Denman faced in the Aon Chase last weekend, Kauto Star dismissed the top-class Monet's Garden and Racing Demon, the performance convincing William Hill to cut the defending champion to 8-11 favourite (from 10-11) and leave Denman at 7-4.

Nicholls said after the race: 'I don't think I have ever been so nervous as I have been this week. I didn't even watch too much of it.

We wanted him to win like he did today. There was a lot not in his favour round here by racing right-handed and over a trip short of three miles.

'I think he is as well as he has ever been, if not better. He looks great, we've left plenty to work on again but he is probably a lot fitter than Denman because he is that type of horse.

'It's always difficult to pick one. I have a certain amount of loyalty to him because he is the reigning champion, but you could see on today's performance he is going to be very hard to beat.

'It's great to have two good chances that seem to be way above the rest of the opposition at this moment.'

After last year's scare in which Kauto Star was pushed to the line by L'Ami in his Gold Cup prep race in the Aon Chase, Nicholls had been determined to have his horse readier for the more searching examination of yesterday's Grade 1 prize.

Ruby Walsh settled in third behind the strong gallop set by Fair Along but though Monet's Garden closed on them to eyeball the favourite at the fourth-last, Kauto Star asserted from the next to finish comfortably in charge.

'He was brilliant,' Walsh said. 'He did exactly what I wanted him to do and I didn't have to give him a belt or anything.

'The Aon Chase was a pretty uncompetitive race. This was competitive and a true-run race. After what Denman did last week you hoped he could do this. I hope to God the two of them get there because it will be some race.'

Clive Smith was equally jubilant: 'He couldn't do any better, could he? He is a remarkable horse. I'm just so excited to have such a good horse. He is such an athlete.'

It was a crucial 24 hours for Kauto Star, and Alastair Down was one of many hoping he would make it to Prestbury Park:

All we were praying for was a clear run through to Cheltenham for Kauto Star and Denman for the most anticipated jumps clash in a generation, but the dream of the head to head looked to be in doubt last night just hours after last year's Gold Cup winner had completed his public prep with a nigh flawless display at Ascot.

In these days of the exchanges, money doesn't talk, it screams out its message. Suddenly early in the evening Kauto Star acquired the leper's bell in the market as the cry went up 'unclean' and punters were suddenly all over Denman like a rash.

If it is a sprained fetlock it is one of those 'how long is a piece of string?' injuries. It is quite impossible to say at this early stage the length of time it will take Kauto Star to recover. In some minor cases it can be eight to ten days, but equally as the extent of the injury becomes clear it might put the Gold Cup favourite out for the season.

One thing is for sure, the horse is in the hands of a man who, more than any other trainer in the country, is an open book when it comes to keeping the public informed about his horses and we know he will tell it like it is.

Of course nobody has died, but the early-evening drama is tooth-grindingly frustrating and nowhere will the possibility of the Denman–Kauto Star clash failing to materialise be felt more sharply than by the staff at Ditcheat. But should this once-in-a-generation showdown be denied to us, the disappointment across racing will be profound.

Not since the early 1960s has a race been so keenly anticipated or the build-up to it seemingly been so perfect. All season, like grizzled poker players on a river boat all of their own, the two horses have continually upped the ante. The first massive raise in stakes came from Denman when he shredded his Hennessy field, flicking off top weight in a way that showed the raw power was underpinned by real class.

Then Kauto Star fired his own broadside in return with a dazzling King George that put him firmly back as ruler of the roost. Just last weekend Denman turned a four-horse race into something both special and full of portent. He blew like a forge bellows afterwards and every fibre of him told you there was more to come.

Yesterday Kauto Star unsheathed the stiletto of his brilliance once more, sliding it between the ribs of the Denman camp with an effortless victory that showed that there is no pace that can be gone that he won't be able to live with.

This is the horse who won a Tingle Creek en route to a Gold Cup and every time Ruby Walsh squeezed him up you could see Kauto Star 'find'. The wining margin of eight lengths could easily have been 18.

Now the high hopes for a race of races on March 14 hang on a thread in the breeze and it is a sickener. Even if Kauto Star's injury is not bad, we are looking at an interrupted preparation at the very best and the chance to give the wider sporting public an event that could set fire even to a non-racing imagination will be lost.

Speculation is something best left to overpaid fat cats in the City; all we can do is hope that as scares go this one is next to nothing. But it will have to be just that if Kauto Star is to run at Cheltenham because nobody can expect connections to send him there anything less than 100 per cent.

Incidentally the injury did not come as a bolt from the blue to all at Ascot as the experienced horsewoman with whom I travelled to the course had already told me Kauto Star was holding a hind leg off the ground in the winner's enclosure.

Let's just hope that all is well but experience and the sheer lack of time between now and Gold Cup day suggest that while the great climax to this season is not sunk as yet, it is undoubtedly holed below the waterline.

As the racing world held its breath, Nicholls announced the next day that Kauto Star was fine and the sport was all set for a mouthwatering Gold Cup, as Rodney Masters reported:

After 14 hours of anxiety and no sleep for Paul Nicholls, Kauto Star was looking in better shape than his trainer last night. He was sound again when led out for a 20-minute walk in the Somerset sunshine yesterday, and his Totesport Cheltenham Gold Cup challenge is back on schedule.

The champion trainer was confident the pus-filled infection within Kauto Star's off-hind foot will have cleared within 48 hours, but the title-holder has not entirely regained his dominance at the head of the market for the March 14 showdown. He was 10-11 with William Hill, but Ladbrokes and Stan James had him sharing favouritism at 5-4 with stablemate Denman.

Nicholls said: 'What happened was similar to a human suffering with a tooth abscess. It can be very painful indeed until the pressure is released. That's why Kauto Star was so lame until the shoe was

removed. When they are that sore, you're always windy as to what the trouble might be.

'The problem had probably been brewing, and the race brought it out. It's by no means uncommon, and if it happens 48 hours before a race the problem can often be sorted out within 24 hours, with the horse sound by the time of the race. However, we would have been in some trouble if this had flared up on Friday night because he'd have missed his final prep.

'When he arrived home on Saturday night our worries were eased because he was obviously more comfortable after the shoe was removed. We were fairly confident by then that it was something simple, but even so, I got very little sleep because there's always a worry what I might find in the morning. I was rather nervous when I came into the yard.'

At his pre-Cheltenham press day Nicholls said that Kauto Star was 100 per cent for the Gold Cup. Lee Mottershead reported from Ditcheat:

Any lingering doubts about Kauto Star's wellbeing were dispelled yesterday after the Gold Cup favourite cantered up trainer Paul Nicholls' uphill gallop showing no sign of the lameness that on Saturday night triggered fears for his Cheltenham challenge.

On a day when Denman's joint-owners Harry Findlay and Paul Barber identified a potential stamina hole in the horse they hope to defeat on March 14, Kauto Star resumed his build-up to the Gold Cup four days after his sparkling Ascot Chase success.

Nicholls said: 'He had a shoe put on this morning and then cantered without any problem at all. He has missed absolutely no work and done everything he would have done even without what happened over the weekend.

'It was the sort of thing that happens to horses in training all the time. Normally, we wouldn't have even said anything and instead just waited a couple of days for it to clear up.'

Nicholls' head groom Clifford Baker, who rode Kauto Star in his canter, added: 'He was great, 100 per cent. He just did one canter up the hill, which is what we would have planned to do with

him anyway. He felt the same as he always feels and there wasn't
anything different about him at all.'

*As the build-up continued the rivalry between Nicholls' two stars was
growing, and Totesport even commissioned a bus to tour the country
and promote the event.*

*The Gold Cup had developed into something special and the racing
public joined in, as David Lawrence reported:*

Whatever reaction passing motorists and pedestrians have to Totesport's
Gold Cup 'battle bus', publicity in the run-up to the Cheltenham Festival
clash is guaranteed the length and breadth of Britain.

Totesport have commissioned a specially designed
election-style double-decker bus to tour Britain to promote the
showdown between Kauto Star and Denman in 18 days' time.

The bus will be fitted with a loudspeaker, through which recorded
audio support for the two Paul Nicholls-trained stars, together with a
boxing-style introduction to their match-up, will be broadcast.

Punters will be able to win a free bet on the race by going to an internet
microsite and confirming where and when they spotted the bus.

The bus will be unveiled on the Friday before the festival, March 7,
before embarking on a tour taking in city centres and racecourses. Its
journey will end on the day of the big race, March 14, when it will be
parked outside the Centaur at Cheltenham.

Punters will be able to board the bus to watch video action of the
Gold Cup's main protagonists on plasma screens, before deciding
which horse they want to support.

In a separate initiative by Cheltenham, rosettes in the racing
colours of the two horses' owners will also be sold on Gold Cup day.

Totesport spokesman Damian Walker said yesterday: 'This is like
the Beatles v the Stones, and the more interest we can drum up for
the Kauto Star v Denman showdown, the better.

'We want to let as many people as possible know about the race, and
we thought an election-style bus would be a good way of doing it.

'People can decide whether they are with the champ or the
challenger – and we want to encourage them to nail their colours to
the mast.'

Sam Thomas and Ruby Walsh in front
of the Gold Cup 'battle bus'

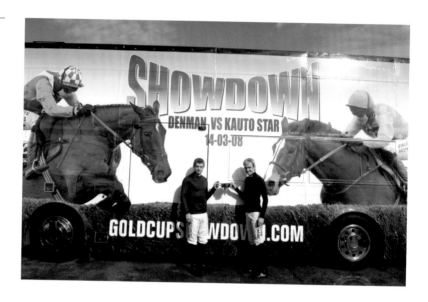

*Clifford Baker spoke to Ben Newton about how much he was enjoying his
involvement with the two superstars a week before the start of the festival:*

During his 32 years in racing, Clifford Baker has been closely
associated with three Gold Cup winners – Charter Party for his
former boss David Nicholson, and See More Business and Kauto
Star during his 12 seasons as head lad to Paul Nicholls. He has also
ridden other champions, such as Azertyuiop and Viking Flagship, but
the situation he finds himself in right now is unique.

'You don't have many horses through your hands good enough to
win a Gold Cup,' he says. 'But to have two at the same time, as we
do, is unreal. To think racing may have not one, but potentially two
superstars on its hands . . .'

For the best part of four seasons, Baker has ridden out the reigning
champion most mornings, but he is keen to stress: 'There is no
favouritism. Whether it's Kauto, Denman or the others, they get the
same treatment from me, and it worries me that people may think
I'm concerned only for Kauto. As long as one of ours wins the Gold
Cup, that's all I care about, and that all the horses come back safe.'

Baker's phlegmatic, feet-firmly-on-the-ground attitude used to
provide the perfect antidote to Nicholls' formerly more combustible
approach. The contrast is less evident nowadays, but Baker has been

there and done it before, and the respect for his methods, and his viewpoint, is widespread.

'With Denman,' he argues, 'we don't know how good he is, because nothing has taken him on this season. That's what makes this Gold Cup so much more exciting.

'Everywhere I go I get asked the same question: which horse is going to win? I'd be a brave man to say definitely Kauto, or definitely Denman, because you can make a strong case for each. If Kauto is lucky enough to win again, I don't think Denman will be far behind him.'

His admiration for Kauto Star, the horse he has long considered to be a 'horse in a million', is boundless. He says: 'It would have been hard to predict Kauto could improve after last season, but in my opinion he has. His last two wins, at Kempton and Ascot, were the best he's ever been, and neither race suited him, being on a right-handed track over a trip short of his best. I agree with Paul: Cheltenham is his ideal track.

'He is now looking like the horse with no flaws – touch wood. Unlike last season, this time I haven't seen him make one serious mistake.'

At Nicholls' recent press day, Baker looked on with interest when Denman's two owners, Paul Barber and Harry Findlay, upped the ante. 'They are looking for any possible chink in Kauto's armour,' he says, 'and if they think it comes down to stamina, that's their opinion.

'But I have never had any doubt about Kauto Star's stamina. And whatever the ground, I don't think either horse will be favoured. People say soft ground could swing it Denman's way, but he is no more likely to stay in a bog than Kauto.'

He rounded off our conversation on a note of caution. 'I hope the contest lives up to all the hype. So often something happens that prevents these big clashes from fulfilling expectations, but it's been a long time since followers of the sport have been able to get their teeth into a race like this, so I hope they won't be disappointed.'

Clive Smith was confident that Kauto could retain his Gold Cup crown, saying: 'I think I'm even more confident than I was last season. I went a little quiet when it looked like the going could get very soft, but I now think that everything is coming in our favour.'

Gold Cup day arrived, but as Alastair Down reported, it was not to be Kauto's day, as Denman put in an unforgettably brutal performance to take his next-door neighbour's crown:

In the end it proved a triumph for substance over style. From the moment Sam Thomas hoisted the 'take no prisoners' flag as he sent Denman into the lead going away from the stands, you had that gut feeling that the big horse, boldness itself as he took huge, effortless cuts at his fences, was not going to be denied.

It was Hennessy afternoon back in December when this huge, rough-cut diamond began to be polished into something close to flawless. With 11st 12lb on his broad back, he put up a handicap performance that sent shivers back through the record books to some of the weight-carrying performances of the 1960s.

The Newbury victory in itself didn't make him Kauto Star's equal, but it was so drenched in possibility, smacked so palpably of greatness within reach, that you knew, in time, he could prove the best from the west. The word I used to describe what he did to his Hennessy field was 'brutalised', and that quality of mercilessness was here in spades once more as he flicked round Cheltenham in full sail.

And this is a horse to whom the public will warm. They will latch on to his size and the stark simplicity of how he goes about his job, the remorselessness of his gallop and the fact you can almost see him saying 'call that a fence?' as he soars over another one.

Sam Thomas will allow him to be led early on in a race, but he must be itching to let him go and start bossing it. And, of course, a horse taking it up so far from home as Denman did in the Hennessy, and again here, is doing it the hard way. But it is far harder for those trying to reel him in, and a nightmare for pursuing jockeys who are torn between conserving their mounts and trying to give chase – an order that is simply too tall.

Jumping lay at the heart of this result. While Denman was swaggering up front, Kauto Star was forever on the back foot. He didn't make a serious mistake, but he didn't jump with any fluency

CHELTENHAM, 14 March 2008		
Totesport Cheltenham Gold Cup Chase	3m2½f	
1 Denman	9-4	S Thomas
2 Kauto Star	10-11f	R Walsh
3 Neptune Collonges	25-1	M Fitzgerald
12 ran 7l, sh hd		

Denman (left) powers home at Cheltenham leaving Kauto Star (right) and Neptune Collonges in his wake, 14 March 2008

and, three or four times, as Denman popped another length up his sleeve, Kauto Star was simply pulling another handful out of an energy bank already under serious strain from the leader's inexorable gallop.

It was clear to the rapt stands from five out that Kauto Star was fraying at the edges, but to my eye Ruby had not been happy for a long time by then. So much of Ruby's strength is unseen as those powerful legs do the work, but he can't have felt he had a prayer from the best part of a circuit from home.

Indeed, given Kauto Star was not at his best, it speaks a vast amount for his sheer class that he narrowed the gap to seven lengths at the line. It may sound madness to some, but for me Kauto Star emerged with his reputation intact and arguably enhanced, because he showed the utmost courage not to flinch in what must have been a searingly hard and lung-shredding pursuit of a horse gone beyond recall.

Kauto Star's performance was below his imperious best, but that must have something to do with the way Denman went about putting this field to the sword. When he is steaming away up front, seemingly without a bother on him, he is forcing all his pursuers to the edge of their comfort zone. They are always having to try to go that half-yard quicker and get that extra momentum at their fences.

Often you hear of jockeys giving their horse a breather, letting those lungs fill, but Denman's gallop rules such luxuries out of court. When he is firing away, he is unrelenting and the lungs of his rivals empty, leaving about as much oxygen as at the top of Everest.

A dejected Ruby Walsh after finishing second to Denman on Kauto Star in the 2008 Gold Cup

But maintaining the power surge out in front is hard labour by any standard, and Denman was mighty tired on the long hill home. But again, you cannot but admire a horse who gives so much of himself, answers every one of Thomas's calls and still keeps trying to find more.

Those who watched this race will not forget it. For sheer destructive, aggressive power, it was a joy to witness. It wasn't pretty but it was definitely handsome. Great chasers must jump, gallop and stay – it's not a complicated cocktail, but it is oh-so-rarely mixed to perfection as it was here yesterday.

A word has to go to both sets of owners. Clive Smith took it on the chin and knows there will be other days for Kauto Star. Paul Barber has been unshakeable in his faith that his horse could win the Gold Cup, and Harry Findlay is simply a lion for Denman, a madly enthusiastic, roaring boy of a jumps nut who brilliantly made his point that this game had been played out straight and honourably in a massive day for the sport.

And Paul Nicholls has also answered every call in the build-up to this epoch-defining race. All those associated with these two mighty horses at Ditcheat have played a massive part in this race.

Although understandably disappointed, the Kauto team were already eyeing a rematch the following season, as Lee Mottershead reported:

Gracious in defeat, eager for the rematch. Ruby Walsh and Clive Smith may have lost the race, but in Kauto Star they have not lost the faith.

In the clash of the titans, it was Kauto Star who came up short, the former champion succumbing to the raw power and irresistible brute force of all-the-way hero Denman.

At the line, seven lengths separated the next-door neighbours, but only a short head prevented the Paul Nicholls third string Neptune Collonges from overhauling Kauto Star. If truth be told, Kauto Star was a beaten horse before the most exhilarating Gold Cup of the modern era had even entered its closing stages.

A steady stream of clumsy leaps hindered his progress, while Walsh was riding hard in advance of the fourth-last fence. To his credit, the eight-year-old stayed on all the way to the winning post, but defeat was utterly comprehensive.

Paul Nicholls with his Gold Cup 1-2-3, Denman (centre), Kauto Star (left) and Neptune Collonges on the day after the race

'The best horse on the day won,' said Walsh.

'Sam picked it up at the first down the back straight, and I knew I couldn't get to him at that stage. Denman was going a good gallop, but no quicker than the horses in the Tingle Creek two years ago, and you'd be hoping that Kauto should have been able to travel, but he didn't.'

Walsh added: 'I could only ride one. I picked the wrong one, and that's racing. The best horse on the day won, but Kauto Star could come back next year – on any given day, any horse can win.'

A positive attitude also emerged from Smith, whose star is quoted at 7-2 by sponsors Totesport to next year exact Gold Cup revenge on the firm's even-money favourite Denman. Cashmans, however, dismissed Kauto Star by issuing an 8-1 price about him for the 2009 edition.

'I think we'll have him in the rematch in 12 months' time,' said Smith.

'Kauto wasn't going a mile from home, so he couldn't have been quite right. He just didn't run his race, but there are no excuses. They're not machines, are they?

'They said that if Kauto could win today, he would be ranked with the all-time greats. Maybe he will next year. He will be back.'

However, the season was not over, as Kauto had a date at Aintree in the Totesport Bowl, and Nicholls was confident he could put his Gold Cup defeat behind him. The race did not go his way, though, as Kauto made an almighty blunder at the second-last which enabled Our Vic to offer a renewed challenge and get up on the line to win by a nose.

Plenty were ready to write him off after a second successive defeat, but Alastair Down was not one of them:

Three weeks ago, Kauto Star ruled the staying chase roost, with just the large and ominous tank that is Denman parked on his lawn and in need of removal in order to maintain his pre-eminence. Two runs and two defeats later, the lustre of last year's Gold Cup winner now carries a trace of tarnish.

It is in the nature of things racing that some folk will start treating Kauto Star like an ageing relative in decline, the glory days gone and a gentle slide down the pecking order some sort of inevitability. No insurance assessor ever declared a write-off quicker than a punter on the wrong end of a couple of reverses.

But the simple truth is that Kauto Star beat himself in the Gold Cup, with the coffin built by his sloppy jumping having the nails hammered home by the remorseless power of Denman. Yesterday Kauto Star made a race-losing mistake when six lengths ahead two from home, and his downfall at the hands of the gallant Our Vic was aided and abetted by Paul Nicholls, who said afterwards that he gave the wrong orders to Ruby Walsh.

If scowls could kill, then several thousand racegoers would have died as Ruby returned to unsaddle with a face you never tire of running away from. Nicholls conceded Ruby was 'mad at me and steaming. He said 'I should have hung on to him and normally I'd have the balls to do what I want', but more times than not we get it right'.

Cross though Walsh may have been with orders that went wrong on him, he will have been far more furious that he didn't just ignore them and do his own thing. But we are all master tacticians after the event.

Up until the festival, it looked as if Kauto Star's jumping had reached a new level of efficiency, with the old trademark errors

AINTREE, 3 April 2008		
Totesport Bowl Chase		3m1f
1 Our Vic	9-1	T Murphy
2 Kauto Star	4-7f	R Walsh
3 Exotic Dancer	6-1	AP McCoy
5 ran nose, 14l		

ironed out. But there is no point pretending that in his last two runs his jumping has not been a significant contributor to his defeats. This observation will be a red rag to Nicholls, but he didn't jump well enough to win a Gold Cup, and his howler here cost him a stack of ground in a race in which he went down by the new minimum of a nose.

To be fair, he didn't look like falling at Cheltenham, but it took an ocean-going error to deck one at the festival, with the percentage of fallers to runners down 50 per cent compared with the last five years.

The bookmakers overreacted. Denman went a shade of odds-on with the Tote for next year's Gold Cup, and Kauto Star is now a general 5-1, with Cashmans going a positively silly 7-1. I am a Denman man to the marrow, but I have admired few performances more in recent years than that of Kauto Star in last month's Gold Cup, when pure class and courage saw him through a sea of troubles to finish a very honourable second.

Nicholls took this reverse well enough, masking his frustration and disappointment a whole load better than the rest of us would. What will stick in the Ditcheat craw is that Kauto Star hasn't ended the season on a high. Those who start to mark him down in their estimation should let their minds wander back to King George day at Kempton, when he was a joy to behold. If he starts next season with a bit of a point to prove, that will only add to the richness of the mix as we build to another Gold Cup confrontation. Denman fans will sleep even easier in their beds, but the legion of Kauto Star supporters shouldn't waver in their faith. But I know which one I would want to jump a fence in order to save my life.

After a pair of disappointing defeats it was time for Kauto Star to go for his summer break, before attempting to become the first horse in the long history of the Cheltenham Gold Cup to regain the title.

5

Regaining the crown

Previous spread: Kauto Star makes history by becoming the first horse to reclaim the Cheltenham Gold Cup, 13 March 2009

THE PREVIOUS SEASON had ended in disappointment as Kauto Star failed in his attempt to retain the Gold Cup, but he had lost nothing in defeat to stablemate Denman. Nicholls said in September that he expected Kauto to prove a major player again and that he would love to win a third King George with the eight-year-old.

In a departure from previous seasons Kauto reappeared at Down Royal, a first appearance away from Britain since his arrival from France in the summer of 2004. In Northern Ireland Kauto Star put down an early marker for the new season, as Lee Mottershead reported:

The old aura of invincibility has returned. Not so long ago, it seemed impossible to imagine how Kauto Star could be bettered, how any staying chaser could have aspirations to be his superior. Then along came Denman, the boy next door, who at Cheltenham last March turned once conventional wisdom on its head. However, based on what we saw yesterday, the old certainties of the past could once again be proved right at Cheltenham next March.

No horse has ever regained the Gold Cup, but Kauto Star started the season in which he seeks to do just that with the greatest possible statement of intent. The JNwine.com Champion Chase was not the finest Grade 1 he has ever contested, but even if The Listener's limp effort turned the task into little more than a penalty kick, Kauto Star could not have converted it more exquisitely.

Pure and simple, he was never out of second gear. Winning as easily as a 2-5 favourite should, he carried Ruby Walsh and a brand-new noseband to a dazzling 11-length defeat of the grossly outclassed Light On The Broom, with Knight Legend a further 11 lengths back in third. In front soon after the third-last fence, he quickly pulled clear, so much so that he was eased down almost as soon as the final obstacle had been jumped.

'He was awesome,' was the initial reaction of Paul Nicholls, and bookmakers seemed to agree. Ladbrokes halved the eight-year-old to 2-1 from 4-1 for the race that matters most. Gold Cup sponsors Totesport went 5-2 from 100-30, while VCbet pushed out

DOWN ROYAL, 1 November 2008		
JNwine.com Champion Chase		3m
1 Kauto Star	2-5f	R Walsh
2 Light On The Broom	50-1	M Walsh
3 Knight Legend	11-1	A Leigh
5 ran 11l, 11l		

Denman, not due to race until February following treatment for a heart problem, to 6-4 from 11-10. The same firm go 4-5 from 5-4 about Kauto Star winning a third consecutive King George VI Chase on Boxing Day, while race sponsors Stan James go even money.

'He travelled well, jumped well and did it all very easily,' said Nicholls. 'He wasn't blowing one iota after the race. He didn't do a thing. He's such a good horse when he's right.

'I was very nervous before the race, but I'm very happy now, mostly for the horse. He got a bit of stick last season, but he still ran some great races. Now he's back to his best.'

Nicholls, who explained that Kauto Star had been fitted with the noseband in a bid to increase his concentration, confirmed that Haydock's Betfair Chase in three weeks' time will be next. Also sure to be at Haydock is owner Clive Smith, who attended Down Royal on crutches after an attempt to jump the Swilcan Burn at St Andrews ended in agony. Smith suggested his horse – looked after yesterday by his new groom Nick Child – looks 'better than ever this year'.

Walsh, who passed the post sporting the same grin he wore when Kauto Star first displayed his brilliance in the 2006 Betfair Chase, certainly seemed to agree. 'I couldn't be happier,' he said. 'He travelled super. Last year I was always squeezing him, even the day he won at Ascot. I never once had to settle him last year, but today I didn't get him to relax until after the fourth-last.'

The Betfair Chase was billed as a rematch between Kauto Star and Exotic Dancer after the pair had been separated by just half a length 12 months earlier. Sam Thomas was back on board again as the luckless Ruby Walsh was injured, but things went awry, as Lee Mottershead reported:

There had, admitted Paul Nicholls in the moments following the Betfair Chase, been many 'ups and downs' in the career of Kauto Star. What we saw yesterday was undoubtedly one of the downs, but the champion trainer left Haydock far from dejected and completely confident his superstar chaser can again deliver Christmas cheer at Kempton next month.

HAYDOCK, 22 November 2008			
Betfair Chase		3m	
1	Snoopy Loopy	33-1	S Durack
2	Tamarinbleu	25-1	T O'Brien
3	Exotic Dancer	7-2	AP McCoy
UR	Kauto Star	2-5f	S Thomas
6 ran ½l, 2¾l			

Kauto Star (left) works with Big Buck's at Ditcheat

For Peter Bowen, Seamus Durack and all associated with 33-1 rank outsider Snoopy Loopy, this was a victory as wonderful as it was unexpected.

However, most of the post-race discussions centred on whether Kauto Star would have secured a Haydock hat-trick but for unseating Sam Thomas at the last when seemingly poised to overhaul gutsy leader Tamarinbleu.

The irony was that the 2007 Gold Cup hero was flawless at the fence itself. Rather, it was after the obstacle had been cleared that the 2-5 favourite stumbled, then slithered, in the process passing up his chance of winning a race he had already almost thrown away when making a mess of the third-last.

Yet even had he won, he would have been unimpressive. In a race in which Tamarinbleu was gifted a soft lead, Kauto Star began to be niggled at soon after heads were turned for home. From that point on, it was courage, not his class, that kept him in contention, just as it was courage that got Snoopy Loopy past Tamarinbleu a mere handful of strides before the line. Half a length separated first and second, with two and a quarter lengths back to Exotic Dancer in third.

Bookmakers immediately made their feelings clear. King George VI Chase sponsor Stan James lengthened Kauto Star's Kempton odds to 6-4 from 4-5. Most of the major firms now have Clive Smith's chaser at 4-1 for the Gold Cup, whose market is dominated by stablemate and title-holder Denman, who is down to evens with Ladbrokes.

'That's racing,' said Nicholls, who confirmed Kauto Star to be '100 per cent' after the race. 'They're horses and they can't be at their very best every single day. Kauto has had his ups and downs in the past, but he bounces back.'

He added: 'I've now got a gut feeling that he's best with his races spaced out and going to those races really fit after lots of work at home.

'It's also true that Ruby knows him better than anyone. Sam had only ridden him once before today, so it's awfully hard for him.'

It seemed remarkable that owing to one error, Kauto was lengthened to odds against for a third King George crown, but Paul Nicholls made it clear the following day that he had no concerns about his superstar.

Kauto Star wears a noseband for the first time for Paul Nicholls in the Champion Chase at Down Royal, 1 November 2008

'I certainly haven't lost any faith in him,' he said. 'What you have to remember is that he was all out to win last year's Betfair Chase but was then awesome in the King George.

'The times to have him at his very best are for Kempton and Cheltenham.

'My job now is to get him back to his very best for Kempton, and I will be doing my best to achieve that.'

Kauto Star and Sam Thomas part company in the Betfair Chase at Haydock Park, 22 November 2008

Asked by the BBC about claims that Kauto Star might be past his best, Nicholls replied: 'I have never heard such rubbish. We should be enjoying horses like this, not knocking them. As soon as people realise they can't win every time – that it's a horserace, and that they are not machines – the better.'

Reflecting on Saturday's race, Nicholls said: 'Hindsight is a wonderful thing, and if Sam could ride the race again, he would have sat two lengths off Tamarinbleu and then kicked on up the middle of the track at the top of the straight.

'It was very difficult for Sam, though, as he'd ridden the horse only once before. He faced an incredibly hard job on Kauto.

'Ruby knows the horse well and he'll hopefully be back for the King George.'

Describing Kauto Star's condition as 'absolutely fine', Nicholls added: 'My head lad Clifford Baker led him out this morning and said he was 100 per cent fine, but just a little bit sore around the hind quarters, which is not surprising when you look at the picture of him on the front page of the *Racing Post*.

'He will have a little physio and be given an easy two weeks before we tune him up for the King George.'

Nicholls urged punters to put a line through the Haydock race and back Kauto at Kempton, saying: 'Nothing would give me more pleasure this Christmas than to see Kauto Star go out and win his third King George. As he's working every bit as well as he was before winning last year, if you can get 11-8 my advice is to lump on!

'He's in great order. After Ruby schooled him last week, the smile he wore said it all. I know Kauto didn't beat much when he won at Down Royal last month, but it was enough to convince Ruby the horse is as good as ever. And that's what he's telling us at home; the piece of work he did the other day with Tatenen, who is favourite for the Arkle, and another with Pierrot Lunaire on Wednesday, told me everything I wanted to know.'

At Kempton, Kauto Star rewarded Nicholls' faith and joined Wayward Lad as a three-time winner of the race – just one behind Desert Orchid – as Jon Lees reported:

Three kings at Christmas. They never miss a nativity and Kauto Star didn't let his audience down on one of racing's biggest stages when he secured his own place in history at Kempton yesterday.

Only two other horses had captured the Stan James King George VI Chase three times, and witnessing Kauto Star join Desert Orchid as one of two to lift the prize on three consecutive occasions yesterday was to be present at a reaffirmation.

This year had previously failed to reach the levels of 2007, when Kauto Star claimed the Gold Cup. Despite two Grade 1 victories, he lost his Cheltenham crown to Denman, was beaten at Aintree, and unseated his jockey after slipping in the Betfair Chase.

Yet trainer Paul Nicholls and owner Clive Smith questioned why anyone had begun to doubt their horse as Kauto Star ended the year showing all his former pomp as he beat Albertas Run by eight lengths, in the process landing a major gamble for Christmas holiday punters.

He is now a top-priced 3-1 (from 5) with Coral and Blue Square for the Gold Cup, for which Denman was eased to 7-4 (from 11-8) by Paddy Power.

No horse has ever reclaimed the Gold Cup, but after yesterday's performance Smith was confident, saying: 'If we get better ground, we'll beat Denman.'

Yesterday Ruby Walsh, absent through injury when Kauto Star failed to complete under Sam Thomas at Haydock on his previous start, never had him further back than fifth. They had a trouble-free passage and when Walsh moved up to tackle the leader, Imperial Commander, after four out, he was full of confidence.

Tony McCoy attempted to make a race of it on Albertas Run, but a fine leap three out sealed the outcome and, despite brushing the final fence, Kauto Star came home in commanding fashion. Albertas Run finished half a length ahead of third-placed Voy Por Ustedes.

Kauto Star, sent off at 10-11 having been available in the morning at 6-4, provided Nicholls with reason to feel vindicated, although as a result of the horse's defeats he has learned Kauto Star needs more time between races nowadays to be at his best.

'I made an error of judgement running him at Haydock last time and I know he wasn't at his best,' he said. 'It wasn't Sam's finest

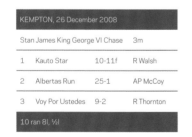

KEMPTON, 26 December 2008		
Stan James King George VI Chase	3m	
1 Kauto Star	10-11f	R Walsh
2 Albertas Run	25-1	AP McCoy
3 Voy Por Ustedes	9-2	R Thornton
10 ran 8l, ½l		

hour. No-one knows what the orders were or how I told him to ride. Everyone tends to forget that, and it didn't work out.

'I knew today he was back at his best and he's just proved how good he is. He won't run before the Gold Cup and will probably have one run then before next year's King George. I know now he needs to be fresh and well, and when he's fresh and well he's as good as he has ever been.

'Everyone has been slagging him off. I think in last season's Gold Cup he didn't run lethargically, he didn't run below par – he ran a better race than the year before when he won it.

'If you took Denman out of the race, he would have won nicely. Denman is the only horse he has met in the last two to three years who has been better than him on the day. He's been amazingly tough to come back from those downs. If we get Denman back, we're going to have another fantastic Gold Cup again. It's a big relief. I wanted this more for the horse than anything.'

Kauto Star is 5-2 with Coral to win a fourth King George next year, emulating Desert Orchid, although the grey's quartet were not gained in successive years.

Walsh said: 'He's a star, isn't he? He's always been a wonderful horse, but when you are at the top people want to knock you.

'To win three King Georges is fantastic. He's a great horse and it is a pleasure to have ridden him in so many races.'

Yesterday's achievement alone was enough to move Smith, who said: 'Tears were streaming down my face as he came in. It meant an awful lot.'

Alastair Down said that public faith was rewarded as Kauto Star dispelled the doubters:

Kauto Star demolished the flimsy arguments of his doubters with an exhilarating third King George victory yesterday, fully justifying the almost belligerent pre-race confidence of Paul Nicholls, who was quick to leap to his horse's defence as the 2007 Gold Cup winner stood triumphant in the winner's enclosure.

Nicholls needn't have said anything as Kauto Star had already done all the talking with as stylish a victory as you could wish to

see – he travelled like the best horse in the race, jumped boldly and quickened up in the way that only the class acts can. In fact Kauto Star's incontrovertible superiority made you wonder how it was possible that he travelled to Kempton having been beaten in three of his last four races.

There was a big-race, adrenaline fizz to the early pace, but round this deceptively tricky course, Kauto Star clicked into an easy rhythm, looking the polar opposite to the harried horse who could never get on an even jumping keel as he played catch-up in the Gold Cup.

At two of the fences he took off extravagantly early, and while he made a slight 'it's still me you know' fluff of the last, his jumping overall was as close to flamboyant as makes no odds. This was Kauto Star at his most eyecatching and rewarding to watch.

For some curious reason Kauto Star is a more popular horse with the racing public than he is with the press and pundits. Yesterday both on course and in the shops nationwide, Kauto Star was bulldozed in from the top morning offer of 6-4 to 10-11 by the off. That is a big, ocean-going gamble fuelled by a vast amount of money on a busy Boxing Day, and it was the voice of the people speaking with both heart and wallet.

But the press and pundits marched to a different tune. The Kempton selections box carried in the *Racing Post* gave the views of 14 of the country's leading tipsters and the six votes for Kauto Star were outnumbered by eight fielding against him. It is likely that a straw poll among paying punters on course here would have yielded a big majority in the favourite's favour.

Nicholls has got increasingly aerated recently at what he sees as sniping against his horse. Some would say that he shouldn't take the criticism so personally, but it is that very passion and involvement with his horses that has driven him up the ranks and catapulted him to pre-eminence.

Furthermore, how many trainers would have the honesty or the balls to admit that two of Kauto Star's last three reverses can be put down to trainer error. Nicholls has been adamant in recent days that he should never have run Kauto Star at Haydock last month, something he had already said about the horse's final outing at Aintree last season when he was turned over by Our Vic.

If you were being particularly hard on the trainer you would have to point out that he was also responsible for the Gold Cup defeat by Denman, though that might be taking the blame game too far.

Though very much a Denman man, I was thrilled to see Kauto Star join Desert Orchid and Wayward Lad as the third horse to win the King George more than twice. And while Kauto Star still has miles to go before he can knock on Desert Orchid's door, his Gold Cup definitely gives him the edge over Wayward Lad who always found that Cheltenham hill beyond him.

Kauto's elevation to racing hero was evident when his trainer revealed the amount of fan mail that had arrived at Ditcheat:

Ruby Walsh and Clive Smith after Kauto Star completed a King George hat-trick

In all the years I've been training I've never had so many cards, faxes, texts and emails than I received after Kauto Star won the King George. Can I thank everyone who took the trouble to write. One letter, which summed everything up from my point of view, said: 'Twas the night after Christmas and in a cold corner of Bleak House Ebeneezer Nevison and Jeremiah Segal were dining frugally on tripe, trotters, humble pie and sour grapes.

'Meanwhile, thousands of Kauto Star fans were carousing, downing ale and singing the praises of their National Hunt hero following his historic King George VI Chase win.

'Along with many other scribes, the pair had consigned Kauto to the scrapheap: 'not the same horse', 'lost his shine', 'best behind him'. Thankfully, the magnificent Kauto gave his critics the equine version of a Winston Churchill.

'The last word goes to his proud trainer, who said, 'I wish some people would give the horse the respect he deserves. I'm so pleased for the horse, not anyone else, just him'.'

I need say no more on the matter.

Kauto had his flu jab the day after Boxing Day, and we'll be following our usual routine with slightly fewer runners in the coming weeks as all the horses receive their vaccinations.

Although Kauto was not seen until Cheltenham, his odds for the Gold Cup shortened after his old rival Denman was beaten by Madison Du Berlais at Kempton at the beginning of February on his long-awaited reapperance.

Two weeks later Nicholls warned that Denman 'still had a mountain to climb' if he was to return to the sort of form that saw him crush Kauto at Cheltenham a year earlier. On the other hand, he predicted that Kauto has 'a great chance' of regaining his crown as he was 'in the form of his life'.

'He's as good as he's ever been,' the champion trainer said, 'and after the way he has bounced back from several defeats, not many horses have achieved what he has.

'He's working away beautifully and I can take him to the festival fresh, like he needs to be, which is such a contrast to last year, when I had to get him back after the Ascot Chase. What with his foot problem it wasn't easy for him.

Ruby Walsh puts Kauto Star through his paces at Ditcheat

'Going into his first run this season at Down Royal, we thought he was back to his best, and while he didn't beat much he was very impressive.

'Things didn't work out right at Haydock – it wasn't my finest moment or Sam's, but we all make mistakes.

'Then he was as good in the King George as he's ever been. We know we've got him really well and he has a great chance – he's the one they all have to beat this year'

On Gold Cup day Nicholls was bullish about Kauto's chance of carving his name into the annals of racing:

I am immensely lucky to have five runners in the Gold Cup and will be over the moon if any one of them brings the trophy back to Ditcheat this evening, but the one most likely to deliver has to be

Kauto Star, and if he can do what no horse has done before him – namely win back the Gold Cup crown – I will be so proud.

Like me, Ruby says the stats are there to be beaten. Kauto is fit, he's fresh, he's well, drying ground will be perfect and he's got a massive chance.

He's had a great preparation this year – very different from 12 months ago, when he went to Cheltenham on the back of a run a month earlier in the Ascot Chase and then had a minor foot problem. It meant he didn't go there as fresh as he could have been, and as he's got older I have learned the need to give him a longer break between races and get him race-fit with plenty of graft at home.

His below-par run at Aintree last spring, and another at Haydock this season in the Betfair Chase, had a lot to do with me bringing him back too soon after his previous run. It may have had something to do with why his jumping never got into any sort of rhythm in last year's Gold Cup. That's why we decided to give him a clear run after winning his third King George on Boxing Day, and everything at home has gone to plan. His final piece of work, with Master Minded last Saturday, was the best I've seen from him in a long time.

I find it strange that I still read that Kauto is not at his best at Cheltenham; he's won a Gold Cup and finished second in another – what more can you ask for? He loves Cheltenham, end of story.

Kauto Star galloped into steeplechasing history at Cheltenham with a breathtaking performance, as Jon Lees reported:

They had never enjoyed a better festival but Paul Nicholls and Ruby Walsh still found room to make history when Kauto Star became the first horse to reclaim the Cheltenham Gold Cup yesterday.

Record-breaking hauls at the meeting for a trainer and rider took second billing to Kauto Star's achievement of succeeding where 24 other champions had previously failed.

The names of some of the greats of the sport feature on the list of those vanquished victors – Mill House, Desert Orchid and See More Business among them – and Kauto Star eclipsed them all when he avenged last year's defeat by Denman in front of an ecstatic 64,000-strong audience at the home of jump racing.

CHELTENHAM, 13 March 2009		
Totesport Cheltenham Gold Cup Chase		3m2½f
1 Kauto Star	7-4f	R Walsh
2 Denman	7-1	S Thomas
3 Exotic Dancer	8-1	AP McCoy
16 ran, 13l, 2½l		

In his most dominant display yet he recorded the biggest margin of victory in the Totesport-sponsored race since 1995 and set up a crack next year at matching the feats of three-time Gold Cup winners Arkle and Best Mate.

There was no hint of nervousness among the principals at the prospect of attempting what had never been done before. Nicholls and Walsh were supremely confident and Kauto Star, the horse who had been 'broken' by Denman a year ago, was never in danger of letting them down.

He travelled and jumped supremely well and shook off a surprisingly spirited effort from Denman to win by 13 lengths, the pair this time helping Nicholls to a Gold Cup one-two-four-five, with Neptune Collonges and My Will chasing home third-placed Exotic Dancer.

But for Celestial Halo's neck defeat in the Champion Hurdle, Nicholls and Walsh would have completed a clean sweep of the festival's four championship races, but of all their aspirations this week victory for Kauto Star was what they coveted most.

Walsh, who rode seven winners at the meeting, said: 'It has been one of those weeks where nothing has gone wrong. Coming here the one I wanted to win was Kauto and he has gone and won. I always believed in him and I hoped that the horse I believed in would turn up and show everyone else how good he is and I think he has.

'He is the greatest horse I have ridden – two miles, three miles and now two Gold Cups. He's a wonderful horse.'

Thanks to Master Minded and Kauto Star, owner Clive Smith completed the Champion Chase-Gold Cup double. 'I'm absolutely staggered,' he said. 'What a wonderful performance – the best he has ever run. It's hard to take in all of these things but it's lovely.'

Kauto Star was never far off a pace cut out by Neptune Collonges and when the pressure began to build on the grey with four to jump he and Walsh were breathing down Christian Williams' neck.

Travelling ominously well, Kauto Star leapt to the front at the next and, though Denman followed them through to threaten briefly, Kauto Star drew away and sealed victory with a clean jump at the last. Denman kept going to take second, two and a half lengths clear of Exotic Dancer.

'It was fantastic for Kauto Star and all the connections. It was fabulous to get him to win again like that. I thought he was a good thing, and he jumped well and won well. It was marvellous to see Denman run so well too. What did Paul have – four of the first five? Michael Dickinson had better watch out!'

Martin Pipe, former champion trainer

'Kauto Star came up the hill almost on the bridle and I don't know any other horse who could do that. It was also something very special from Paul Nicholls. He is an extremely good trainer and he and his team deserve all their success.'

Michael Dickinson, former champion trainer

An elated Walsh said: 'I always had faith in him. I know I got it wrong last year when Denman was awesome but when Kauto won at Down Royal I thought this horse was coming back. When he won the King George he was brilliant and going down to Paul's in the mornings I thought he was back to the horse he was two years ago.

'He's an incredible horse. He has speed for two miles, stamina for three and a quarter. I know he has made mistakes in the past but he's a great jumper on the whole. When you want him he sticks his head down, that's the main thing. It's been an amazing week, one I will never forget.'

Nicholls was almost as thrilled by Denman's effort as that by Kauto Star. 'In my mind Kauto was never going to get beat today,' said Nicholls. 'He is very good when he is like that. I knew he was fresh and well. The prep has gone right, everything has gone right and I was looking forward to him doing what he did. He is as good as he's ever been. Denman has astounded me. It reflects well on the whole team.'

Paul Nicholls later described his special affection for Kauto Star:

No matter how many horses I go on to train, Kauto Star will always hold a very, very special place in my affections, and to win a second Gold Cup, to go with his three King Georges and his Tingle Creeks and his Betfair Chases makes him an incredible horse.

I was able to enjoy yesterday's race so much more than last year; you never want to appear too confident beforehand, but I was as sure as I could be that we had him absolutely spot-on. People kept telling me a horse couldn't come back and regain his Gold Cup crown, but the horse doesn't know anything about statistics, and Ruby and I were happy to ignore them.

The one thing I was worried about was how Denman was going to perform, but Sam soon had him just where we planned, so considering all the pressure, I was able to follow the race closely, unlike last year when it was unbearable.

I was as surprised as Ruby that Denman was still going so well on his outside three out, but Kauto just went away from him. I didn't expect him to win by 13 lengths, but what I did know was we had him

Opposite: Ruby Walsh waves his whip with delight after winning the Gold Cup for the second time, 13 March 2009

Kauto Star and Ruby Walsh pull up

right at his very best – the opposite to 12 months ago, when he met Denman on his day of days and Kauto had a bit of an off-day.

I've learned from my mistakes with Kauto, and know not to run him without a decent break beforehand, so as he gets older we'll have to mind him, but there's no reason why we can't bring him back for his fourth Gold Cup. Jumping fans love nothing more than to see a horse like him in action, but three runs a season is enough now.

Alastair Down wrote that Katuo Star had now secured his place among the all-time greats:

On one of jump racing's imperishable afternoons Kauto Star put both his brilliance and resilience forever beyond question with a flawless display that brooked no argument that he belongs among the sport's genuine greats.

Ruby Walsh and Nick Child celebrate
Gold Cup number two

For as long as punters lift pints in pubs, they will talk about the day Kauto Star won back his Gold Cup crown. Gone was the Kauto Star of 12 months ago, replaced by a chaser at his rampant best, measuring fences with a watchmaker's precision and powering along in such a fashion that he was bossing the race throughout.

Here was the horse who has it all at every trip, the Kauto Star who had the pure speed for two Tingle Creeks, the class that has taken the King George three times and the stamina and courage to power home in two Gold Cups. Few indeed are the chasers who can rule all those roosts – precious few, and all the more fabulous for their rarity.

And if on this afternoon of high emotion Kauto Star leapt from the zones of respect and affection to the higher reaches of true attachment and affection, at least part of the feelgood factor generated by this spellbinding race lay in the mighty performance of a resurgent Denman in second place. He jumped with all his old zest and stuck on little less than heroically to hold Exotic Dancer at bay for second.

> **'It was a massive achievement [training Kauto Star to regain the Gold Cup]. It's only when it has happened that you realise how remarkable it was that it never happened before. And there's a chance it could happen again next year with Denman. It was wonderful the way the race unfolded and the reception they received.'**
>
> Edward Gillespie,
> Cheltenham managing
> director

In running such a mighty race, Denman banished the spectre of the out-of-sorts shadow of his former self we saw on his first dismally depressing run of the season.

It was almost like having two Gold Cup results to cheer – Kauto Star winning the day in a league of his own with Denman also a glorious winner, because the big horse won his all-important battle to be back in business.

He came in tired and weary, well ahead of Kauto Star, to a reception that dwarfed that which several winners had received during the week, but it was nothing to compare with the sustained roar of joyous approval that met Kauto Star. With Ruby on top beaming fit to crack a jaw, Kauto Star made his honoured way down the horsewalk in front of stands and lawn that erupted in a heaving, raucous ferment of joyous appreciation.

Up through the paddock he came, king of the Cheltenham hill once more, to enter the winner's enclosure as the first horse ever to regain a Gold Cup crown.

The way we welcome winners at Cheltenham and the ritual of our acknowledgement are not small and insignificant things. You and I don't live with the great horses, see them every morning or walk short yards to rub noses as they poke heads over box doors.

So the great racing public will travel long miles and pay good money to see them fleetingly, or glimpse them via the artificial proximity of the television. But when a Gold Cup winner walks in to stand steaming at the centre of the jumping universe it is our infrequent opportunity to get up close to the animal who has just lifted 60,000 fellow souls aloft and open our throats, long and loud, in thanks. Small wonder we make a big noise.

As Kauto Star powered away from the second-last with the race won and Cheltenham fast approaching the boil, just the final fence – no small peril in races past – lay between him and the door marked 'Legends'. You could see Ruby alert to every signal he was getting, covering every eventuality from clean leap to costly clout, and as the very moment of take-off approached he slapped his ally three times down the shoulder, smacking out the tattoo, 'Get This Right'.

But there was no glitch. Kauto Star slotted the perfect final-fence jump, the last point of drama conquered in a race that had everything.

Rarely, if ever, have I witnessed a race at Cheltenham so perfect as a spectacle and so fulfilling in its result. Paul Nicholls, Ruby Walsh and indeed Clive Smith have enjoyed a week that only the gods could hand out. And while their happiness will be immeasurable and their satisfaction beyond fathom, all of us on hand for the Gold Cup also walk away as winners. Strange as it may sound, the 6min 44sec of yesterday's race added up to one of jumping's finest hours.

And when some cynic tells you that we perhaps invest too much in the Cheltenham Festival, that the hype is overdone and that there are other great racing occasions, then shake your head gently and remind them of this race, on this day, when Kauto Star transformed the making of racing history into something memorably effortless as he galloped and jumped his way into the inner circle of the indisputably special.

Glittering was the crown regained and utterly magnificent the wearer of it.

The place to be the following day was Ditcheat as the village hosted yet another welcome home party for Manor Farm's heroes. Ben Newton was there, with Nicholls already thinking about 12 months time:

Paul Nicholls yesterday ruled out the prospect of Kauto Star running again this season, but said he hoped the dual Gold Cup winner would run in the race in the next three years.

Kauto Star was in rude health after his arrival back at Manor Farm Stables in Ditcheat at 9pm on Friday evening, and was paraded with other members of Nicholls' record-breaking Cheltenham team in the village yesterday.

The nine-year-old is 5-2 with the sponsors Totesport to win a third Gold Cup; William Hill make Nicholls 8-11 to win the race in 2010.

Nicholls said: 'He's such a complete professional, he amazes me. He wins his second Gold Cup like that, hardly has a blow in the winner's enclosure, came back and ate up last night as if he'd just done a normal day's work.

'But Clive Smith and I have had a chat this morning and agreed that he's done enough for the season. A reappearance at Down Royal

'To get Denman back to run like that was amazing, and Kauto Star too. Hats off to Paul. We all know how hard it can be to get just one horse here in one piece. Personally I always thought Kauto Star was the better horse, but it was a fantastic effort from Denman today.'

Nicky Henderson, leading trainer

'Kauto Star is a terrific horse. He looked terrific in the paddock and I wasn't surprised that he won. Paul Nicholls is a brilliant trainer. I take my hat off to him and I congratulate him.'

Trevor Hemmings, owner

Paul Nicholls and Clive Smith hold aloft the Gold Cup the day after Kauto Star's historic triumph

again in the autumn is not set in stone, but that remains the likely starting point.'

Reflecting on Kauto Star's historic achievement in becoming the first horse to win back his Gold Cup crown, Nicholls said: 'It was great to see Kauto on the front page of all the papers this morning, and racing wants to make the most of him. He's only nine.

'He's so well you wouldn't know he'd had a race. But we don't want a repeat of last season, when he got beat at Aintree, and it would ruin the summer if he didn't bow out on a high.

'Friday's win showed he's as good as he's ever been. When he's super-fit and fresh, as he was for this year's race, he's lethal.

'He was in the best shape I've ever had him. I've said all along he's been in better form this season than last, and there's no reason why he can't come back the same in the autumn, as I see no sign of deterioration. And if he has just three runs a season, he could run in the Gold Cup at ten, 11 and 12. With any luck, next year we'll get him and Denman back for the race both in tip-top form.'

Paul Nicholls with his Cheltenham heroes Big Buck's, Master Minded and Kauto Star

He added: 'Kauto worked the Saturday before the Gold Cup with Master Minded, and the Saturday before that with Celestial Halo, and those are both seriously good two-milers. There aren't many Gold Cup winners who could do that – I certainly couldn't do it with Denman or Neptune Collonges.

'Big Buck's is the only other high-class horse in the yard who's a bit like Kauto in possessing that blend of speed and stamina. Over the years there have been plenty of arguments, with people saying Kauto needs to go left-handed or right-handed, and that he doesn't jump, but what he did on Friday must have convinced everyone he's one of the greatest horses we've seen in a long time.'

After Kauto Star's annual summer break Nicholls threw open the doors at Manor Farm at the start of September for his owners' open day, as Ben Newton reported:

Hopes that we could be all set for another vintage jumps season were

Previous spread: Denman and Kauto
Star frolic during their summer holiday

sent sky high yesterday when Paul Nicholls vowed 'to do everything possible to get Kauto Star and Denman back for the Gold Cup next March in the form of their lives'.

A Cheltenham decider between Britain's two champion staying chasers would be the most eagerly awaited clash of the season and 'so good for racing', according to Nicholls, although he warned: 'There are plenty of bridges to be crossed before we get there.'

The score in their Gold Cup head-to-heads is one apiece; Denman thrashed a slightly below-par Kauto Star seven lengths in the 2008 renewal before Kauto, the 2007 winner, got his revenge when regaining his crown last March after it was touch and go whether Denman made the line-up.

The chasing giants were yesterday accompanied by two-mile champion Master Minded when stealing the show at Nicholls' annual owners' open day in Ditcheat, held for the first time in two years after last year's event was abandoned due to flooding.

For the 350 owners and invited guests present, the mere sight of jumping's three top-rated chasers – between them the winners of 19 Grade 1s over fences and £3.43 million in prize money – looking fresh and well, if not yet in the peak of condition, was enough to fuel anticipation that we may be on the verge of another memorable winter.

'Kauto Star looks great,' said Nicholls, 'and is exactly where I want him. But he's had a lot of mileage on the clock since he was three and I've got to look after him from now on. He's best very fit and very fresh, so he may not have more than three or four runs this season.

'He'll start off either in the JNWine.com Champion Chase at Down Royal on November 7, or the Betfair Chase at Haydock a fortnight later. I know I said after last year he wouldn't go to Haydock again, but he's won the Betfair twice already, so I can hardly say he doesn't act round there. But Down Royal is the first option.'

Kauto Star will then bid to become the first horse ever to win four consecutive King Georges. The great Desert Orchid is the only four-time winner of Kempton's Boxing Day showpiece, but that came during a five-year spell between 1986 and 1990 after his sequence was halted when Nupsala beat him into second in 1987.

Kauto Star and his growing list of Grade 1 victories

'For Kauto to win it four times would be unbelievable,' said Nicholls, 'but whatever happens at Kempton we'll then keep him fresh for Cheltenham.'

Two weeks later came the news the dam of Kauto Star had been put down in France at the age of 16.

Kauto Relka injured her spine in a paddock at her breeder Henri Aubert's stud farm near Le Lion d'Angers in western France.

'It has been a dream ride and it is a shame it ends like that but I have been very lucky with her,' Aubert said in a report on frogsracing.com.

'She gave me 13 foals in 14 seasons. She was barren once only because the sire she was supposed to visit got a problem.'

Kauto Relka was produced by a mating of Port Etienne and Kautorette. She never raced but found fame as a broodmare.

Her visit ten years ago to Village Star, who ran fifth in Tony Bin's Prix de l'Arc de Triomphe in 1988, produced a bay colt later named Kauto Star.

Kauto Star began his sixth season of racing in Britain at Haydock when he attempted to win the Betfair Chase for the third time, and Nicholls had him in tip-top shape for the race, but it was a close-run thing, as he only got home by a nose. Tom O'Ryan reported:

It was the sort of thrilling outcome that makes the hairs on the back of your neck stand up.

A blunt knife would have cut the atmosphere at the end of a finish that will live long in the memory. And, as for the cheers that rang out when the result virtually everyone wanted to hear boomed over the Tannoy, they had to be heard to be believed.

For anyone who is passionate about jump racing, Haydock was the place to be yesterday.

Kauto Star, the king, remains very much in residence. In gaining his 19th career win, by a nose from Imperial Commander in the Betfair Chase, he added yet another extraordinary highlight to his dazzling record, and left those who doubted his ability to overcome softer-than-ideal ground eating their words.

Paul Nicholls was thrilled to see his stable star come out on top for the third time in four years in this Grade 1 event, 12 months after unseating Sam Thomas at the final fence.

The trainer said: 'As they went past the line, I couldn't call it. I just didn't know – it was that close. But my immediate feeling was that, win or lose, he'd run a fantastic race.

'That was a great spectacle, and it's great that he's won. I've had one of the most nerve-wracking weeks of my life. For some reason some of my horses have taken a little bit longer to come to hand this season, but he's proved he was fit enough to do the job on the day.'

That said, Nicholls was quick to pass on the post-race analysis of Ruby Walsh, who gave Kauto Star a dynamic ride, in much the same way as Paddy Brennan excelled on the gallant Imperial Commander.

'Ruby said the three most important words I wanted to hear – "He needed it." He's come here and won, but now we know we can improve him. We can fine-tune him and get him ready for the King George and then the Gold Cup.'

HAYDOCK, 21 November 2009		
Betfair Chase		3m
1 Kauto Star	4-6f	R Walsh
2 Imperial Commander	9-1	P Brennan
3 Madison Du Berlais	6-1	T Scudamore
7 ran nose, 24l		

Kauto Star remains 10-11 favourite with Totesport to gain a record fourth consecutive win in the King George, while they cut Imperial Commander to 5-1 (from 14). As for the Gold Cup, Kauto Star is a general 6-4 with Imperial Commander at 10-1.

Given a typically cool ride by Walsh, Kauto Star moved smoothly into contention with a mile to run, by which time Punchestown Gold Cup winner Notre Pere, who eventually finished a remote fifth, was beginning to send out distress signals.

Heading towards the end of the back straight, Imperial Commander had gone to the front, but Kauto Star was firmly in his slipstream and, as Walsh peered backwards between his legs, he realised that a two-horse war was in the offing.

The ensuing battle was the sort to be talked about late and long in bars everywhere, fought out by two brave horses and two brilliant jockeys.

Nicholls was proud of Kauto Star, who is six weeks short of his tenth birthday and was having his 32nd start.

'To see him, at his age, put his head down and fight like that was something else,' he said.

The last word went to Walsh. In that typical straight-bat style of his, the jockey said of Kauto Star: 'Some people always seem to want to knock this horse, but how many Grade 1s is that he's won now, 12? He's as good a horse as we've ever seen.'

Few at Haydock yesterday would have disagreed.

Alastair Down believed it was a race that should be cherished:

Most races, even those at the highest level, soon slip down between the duckboards of memory, but yesterday's Betfair Chase was an exception, not least because even after it was over it had not finished handing out both drama and surprise.

As Imperial Commander and Kauto Star passed the post locked in combat there were plenty who thought Paddy Brennan had edged it after a no-prisoners duel all the way up the straight. As Ruby Walsh brought Kauto Star back through the paddock towards the unsaddling enclosure ahead of the photo verdict, he shook his head at me in a rueful concession that he had got chinned. After a

Kauto Star keeps Imperial Commander at bay in the Betfair Chase at Haydock, 21 November 2009

gladiatorial struggle it looked as if the Caesars of the photofinish would be giving the Gold Cup winner the thumbs down.

But Kauto Star had edged it in an unflinching set-to that had as-near-as-dammit all one hopes to see in a top-class chase. Those taken aback by the nose verdict against Imperial Commander would have had their minds put at rest by being able to view the actual photo that showed the narrow but palpable margin of victory. But there followed one of those unfunny little comedies when the photo image was nowhere to be seen, though it did eventually appear on Haydock's closed-circuit TV without provoking riots or prompting anyone to torch the stands.

But, of course, reality-challenged conspiracy theorists of the sort who think Elvis is practising as a Presbyterian minister on the Isle of Mull had a field day suggesting on various outlets for the bewildered and forums for the factually challenged that dirty deeds were afoot at the crossroads.

The boring and unvarnished truth is that it was not possible immediately to produce an image that was of sufficient quality to

publish widely. It would have perpetuated confusion rather than brought illumination. At the risk of playing with words, you can have a clear result without it appearing very clear.

Losing rides give the jockey involved no joy, and this was in all likelihood Brennan and the admirable Imperial Commander's best shot at upending Kauto Star, as Kempton's right-handed track will not be as suitable.

Brennan will have been inconsolable, but he rode a masterpiece, making a clearly visible move to nick two lengths at a crucial stage around four from home and somehow getting his mount to regroup and dig yet again when all seemed lost.

But what makes Kauto Star fascinating to watch is the fact that his story continues to unfold and grow in the telling.

It is not a question of revelations, but of a new twist to the plot. We know he is all class and we know he can scrap, but at Haydock yesterday he combined courage and ability in as admirable a way as I have ever seen from him.

And while it will be the Gold Cups and King Georges that the monks illuminate on the record books, anyone here who saw the thrill of the struggle, waited for the result and then had the frisson of the roar that greeted it will not let it go from the mind. This was the sort of performance that gets under the public's skin and lodges in their heart.

What's more, at rising ten years of age, Kauto Star is acquiring the patina of having been about the place for ages. We have Nicholls to thank for the spareness with which he is campaigned, as he is given a racing programme designed to preserve him and not expose him to inevitable wounds of attrition that frequent fighters inevitably incur.

It is not some accident that he became the first horse to reclaim a Gold Cup crown, it is by design – a design by P Nicholls.

Happily, my fellow *Post* scribe has escaped the know-all, know-nothing abuse that Henrietta Knight used routinely to receive for not running Best Mate three times a week when there was an R in the month – a policy that yielded the not-insignificant matter of three Gold Cups.

Nicholls, hugely cheered by the news from Ruby that Kauto Star needed the race, was a man off whom relief ran in rivulets afterwards. We live in an age of instant verdicts and rushed judgements, so just imagine the silly hoo-ha if the photo had gone the other way and both Kauto Star and Master Minded had got beaten in just seven days. 'That Paul Nicholls has gone at the game,' would have been a mere overture to the twaddle-fest.

Thank God we have been spared all the tosh that would have been trotted out by those who can't see the routine without wishing to make something speciously sensational out of it.

Ruby spoke yesterday of 'people knocking Kauto Star all last week'. And if they knock Kauto Star, then shame on them. There is all the difference in the world between the asking of legitimate questions and the finding of artificial fault.

Most of us thought the Betfair Chase was something close to a wonder to behold, one of those races with nearly every ingredient you would expect to find on the tin marked 'Epic Chases'. It was not far off what the sport is always striving to produce and which we live in hope of seeing.

Yesterday, on the flatlands in the lee of the M6, jumping soared beautifully above its unlovely surroundings.

While Kauto Star started the season as he ended the old one, Denman reminded everyone just how good he was with a second outstanding

victory in the Hennessy Gold Cup. The question on everyone's lips was:
Who would you support in March? Lee Mottershead reported:

On good ground, maybe Kauto Star, on soft ground, maybe Denman, but on something in between, who knows?

That was yesterday's assessment from Paul Nicholls, who admitted he has no idea which of his two chasing megastars will emerge victorious in the Totesport Cheltenham Gold Cup.

Kauto Star's owner Clive Smith, however, took slight issue with the assertion by Denman's joint-owner Paul Barber that soft ground would always favour Barber's horse, saying: 'I'm not sure he's right when he says Denman will always beat us in a soft-ground Gold Cup, as Kauto can race in soft ground.'

Smith, whose pride and joy shades Denman for Gold Cup favouritism with most firms, added: 'Kauto probably didn't have his best day when he lost to Denman in 2008, although Denman was exceptional in that Gold Cup and he was outstanding at Newbury in the Hennessy Gold Cup on Saturday.

'It's very difficult to say definitely one thing or another, but I do think it will be a very close-run race at Cheltenham in March.'

Denman's successful shouldering of top weight to a second Hennessy Gold Cup victory has ignited debate about which of the Nicholls stablemates will prove superior when, all things permitting, they clash for the third time for jumping's most prestigious prize.

With each holding one Cheltenham verdict over the other, their latest encounter will be billed as the great decider.

Barber, whose fellow owner Harry Findlay reckons that Denman will prevail whatever the conditions, predicted at Newbury that Kauto Star would win a good-ground Gold Cup, while his horse would score on a soft surface.

Nicholls largely agrees, and said yesterday: 'If the ground is very soft, it would definitely swing Denman's way. If the ground is good, it would swing Kauto's way. If the ground is in the middle, it would be very interesting.

'One horse likes really good ground, one likes really soft, but they both go on either, so if it was midway I wouldn't know what to say. The biggest headache will be Ruby Walsh's, as he'll have to make a decision. It will make things very interesting.'

Stan James yesterday made Walsh 4-7 to side with Kauto Star, and 5-4 to pick Denman. They quote Sam Thomas at 4-9 to ride the horse Walsh does not.

At Newbury, Denman confirmed himself to be over the heart scare that delayed his reappearance last term, producing a flawless exhibition, the only worry coming at the start, where Walsh had to roust the nine-year-old into action.

While everyone else seemed to be concerned only about March, Paul Nicholls was focussed on the task in hand – namely a record-equalling fourth King George to make Kauto Star the first horse to win the race four times in a row.

At Kempton Kauto romped home by 36 lengths, as Jon Lees reported:

A hat-trick of victories was a rare enough achievement, yet the best was still to come from Kauto Star, who secured a unique place in William Hill King George VI Chase history with his greatest performance yesterday.

The formality all 22,000 of Kempton's sell-out Boxing Day crowd had gathered to witness was duly completed, but it was the manner in which he rose to the challenge of bettering Desert Orchid's previously unmatched achievement that took the breath away.

Victories at Kempton over Exotic Dancer, Our Vic and Albertas Run plus two Totesport Cheltenham Gold Cups had established Kauto Star as a special horse but, in becoming the first to clinch four King George VI Chases in a row, he produced a demonstration without parallel and took his prize money earnings past the £2 million mark.

Exhibitions of such perfection are scarce, yet Kauto Star jumped flawlessly as he routed a field of accomplished steeplechasers, finishing 36 lengths clear of Madison Du Berlais and at the same time keeping hopes that he could return for a fifth attempt very much alive.

In a year in which Sea The Stars became the first Flat horse to win the 2,000 Guineas, Derby and Prix de l'Arc de Triomphe and Kauto

KEMPTON, 26 December 2009			
William Hill King George VI Chase		3m	
1	Kauto Star	8-13f	R Walsh
2	Madison Du Berlais	10-1	T Scudamore
3	Barbers Shop	14-1	B Geraghty
13 ran 36l, 1l			

Kauto Star and Ruby Walsh come home in splendid isolation to record a fourth successive King George victory at Kempton, 26 December 2009

Star had already become the first chaser to reclaim the Cheltenham Gold Cup crown, Clive Smith's champion ensured that 2009 ends as one of the most memorable 12 months for the sport of horseracing.

The horse who had scrambled past the finishing post a nose in front of Imperial Commander on his first start since March, in the Betfair Chase at Haydock, proved a very different proposition at Kempton.

Ruby Walsh settled Kauto Star no further back than fourth as Ollie Magern and Nacarat cut out the running and, with Imperial Commander meeting problems early and Deep Purple also struggling, needed only to stay in touch until the pace began to tell on his other rivals.

Nacarat held the lead to the fourth-last but from there the die was cast, Kauto Star producing a superb leap that was the cue to move into the lead.

Clear in the straight, he took the last three fences with aplomb and was cheered to the echo as he was led back to the winner's circle.

Trainer Paul Nicholls said: 'He has saved the best for today. I don't know about going backwards – he seems to be going forwards.

'That was one of his best if not his best ever performance. Everything at home in the last two weeks has suggested it. I knew he would come on a ton from Haydock.

'I have seen some great horses and that is as good as I've seen. The era of Arkle and Mill House was very special but this horse is up there with them.'

Nicky Henderson, leading trainer

'It was a fantastic performance and probably his best. He's just demolished what I thought was a good field. If I went literally through Madison Du Berlais, he comes out about 199, but I'm not going to do that. His previous best was 186, though, and he'll definitely go over that. 190 has a sort of psychological barrier to it, so it's interesting. I'll have another look at the race . . . He was stunning. I've never seen anything better.'

Phil Smith, BHA head of handicapping

'You don't have them at their best on their first run of the season. He has done nothing but improve since then. He would be a hard horse to beat next year. He's just as likely to be back next year if he stays sound because he's not going to have too many runs, we will look after him and that will be the aim. Cheltenham Gold Cup and then back here.

'It's fantastic. I was nervous. I wanted to get him here in the best of form. There was a lot of pressure on everybody. Hopefully he's great for racing and the crowd have got what they wanted to see. The race was never in any doubt, bar an accident. He was always cruising and jumping. Just what Ruby and I talked through happened.'

Joint-favourite for the Gold Cup with stablemate Denman before the race, Kauto Star is now back at the head of the ante-post market, as he was cut to 7-4 favourite (from 9-4) by William Hill, who quote him at 6-4 for next year's King George.

Walsh was not about to confirm his riding plans for the Gold Cup. 'Cheltenham is a long way away and this is King George day,' he said, but he marvelled at Kauto Star's ability to come back year after year.

'He never missed a beat,' the jockey said. 'He was deadly. He's an unbelievable horse. You keep coming back and you think some day he can't be as good, but today he turned up better than ever. He's an unbelievably durable horse. You think of the race he had behind Denman in the Gold Cup, Our Vic at Aintree, and he came back the following year and this year as the horse he is. Desert Orchird was incredible. To win four King Georges one after another is unbelievable.'

Smith said: 'The Gold Cup was fantastic but so was that. He was terrific, absolutely outstanding. I can't think of good enough words to say about him. He was just so, so good. We go for the Gold Cup now very seriously. I'm over the moon.'

The last word on a fourth consecutive King George win for a steeplechaser venturing into magical territory went to Alastair Down:

With a performance raw in its superiority Kauto Star duly landed his fourth consecutive King George yesterday, but his real achievement lay in soaring to a new level of brilliance that opened up fresh frontiers of the achievable.

They had gone a gallop guaranteed to expose weakness, yet as they jumped the second-last Ruby Walsh and Kauto Star were still steaming strongly ten lengths clear of a quality field that had long run up white flags and sued for peace.

It was what happened between the landing side two out and the line that almost beggared belief and smacked the certainty into your psyche that you were lucky enough to have been on hand the afternoon Kauto Star entered territory that, even as a dual Gold Cup winner and three-time King George hero, he had never ventured into before.

Rampant at the last, with the Walsh adrenaline/ecstasy mix coursing to every nerve tip, Kauto Star powered up the short run-in to win by 'a distance' – the measure that traditionally describes margins so enormous as not to be worth quantifying.

My *Post* colleagues assessed the true margin at 36 lengths, and unless you somehow conclude that runner-up Madison Du Berlais, third-placed Barbers Shop and fourth Nacarat were all below par, then Kauto Star has hauled himself to around the 190 mark, which is where the mortals stop and the gods kick in. Head of handicapping Phil Smith, a man paid to be unimpressed, simply said: 'I have never seen better.'

It is almost certainly true that the corking rattle at which Nacarat took this field along simply found out nearly all of them. But the pace didn't lay a glove on Kauto Star; indeed, he thrived on it, because two of the men who know him best, Paul Nicholls and Walsh, were taken aback and in a state of happy shock at the revelation that was this Kauto Star.

In his *Post* column Nicholls had used the expression 'he's lethal' to describe Kauto Star at his peak, and it is hard to think of a word that better describes the almost dangerous quality of this win.

To my eye, this was almost like watching another horse to the one we have got to know so well in recent seasons. Suddenly, a whole new horse and force had been unveiled before us.

Kempton's Boxing Day crowd is a rich mix of racing diehards and folk desperate to escape family festivity. But nobody here yesterday

> **'It was a great performance from a great horse. It was a competitive race and he was always jumping, always travelling. He's beaten everything by a distance. He's definitely up there among the very best.'**
>
> Martin Pipe, former champion trainer

> **'It was a hell of a performance just to get him well enough to come here four times, let alone win.'**
>
> Nigel Twiston-Davies, trainer

'I have just been consoling my seven-year-old daughter, explaining to her that Dessie, who was the first horse she sat on, has lost absolutely nothing, but it's fantastic that Kauto Star won it so brilliantly and both David [Elsworth] and I were cheering him on watching the race on television. Dessie was a fantastic horse and it's great that one has come along who is as good as him in a different way. To win with such authority was a terrific performance, and my congratulations to all concerned. Who can say who would have won had they raced? We have been lucky to have been associated with a great horse and here comes another one, and all power to them. It's great for the sport.'

Richard Burridge, owner of Desert Orchid

could fail to have immediately grasped that they were being handed something utterly special.

Until his regaining of the Gold Cup crown last March, the emotional connection between Kauto Star and the public had always been less than it should have been. But if the stream of affection began to flow on that Friday then the very floodgates opened here, with joyful bedlam reigning as Ruby paraded him in front of the stands and the 'our cheers' that rang out twice for Kauto Star were genuine roars, not whimpers.

Kempton can be a place short on soul, but not this Boxing Day when the crowd who came to see a small but notable record – four consecutive wins – found themselves suddenly borne up in a celebration of something far more rare and wonderful.

Sometimes a crowd can almost miss the true significance of what is laid before them – but nothing was lost in this mix of humanity who gave Kauto Star a reception worthy of the performance.

Here was a staying chaser who we thought we knew backwards producing one of the definitive performances of all time, an effort almost from another dimension. Long after he had been loaded on the bright red box to bear him home, grizzled old race-watchers were still shaking their heads contentedly from side to side wallowing in the magic of this afternoon.

And the fact that this performance came off a gallop of genuine severity will not have been lost on Denman's supporters, because whatever the big horse can do will not inconvenience his next-door neighbour in this sort of form.

What is almost more than any of us deserve is that we have the prospect of a staggeringly exciting third Gold Cup clash in March. We know Denman is back to his best because he has locked a second Hennessy in the cupboard off 11st 12lb and while Kauto Star was a half-brother to a phenomenon here we know he has succumbed to Denman at Cheltenham in the past.

This was one of those days of reward when the soul is nourished and the spirit soars, one for the list of incontrovertibly magical occasions that pepper the lives of those who love watching horses racing in the hope that, every incarnation or so, we are unforgettably visited by the remarkable. As we were at Kempton on this Boxing Day God gave.

Kauto Star was at the height of his powers in 2009 after regaining the Gold Cup and winning a fourth consecutive King George VI at Kempton. Everything was now geared towards attempting to emulate Cottage Rake, Arkle and Best Mate and become a three-time Gold Cup winner.

'He's an amazing horse. In my time he's definitely the best.'

Tony McCoy, multiple champion jockey

6

Decline

Previous spread: A disconsolate
Paul Nicholls, with his then partner
(now wife) Georgie, after Kauto Star
was pulled up in the Punchestown
Guinness Gold Cup, 4 May 2011

Below: Clifford Baker (left) and
Paul Barber admire Kauto Star

Kauto Star was at the top of his game approaching the Gold Cup
and it looked as though 'The Decider', as the race was being billed,
might be a one-horse show after Denman failed to complete in the
Aon Chase at Newbury on his reapperance.

Nicholls was in bullish mood four weeks before the race, as
Ben Newton reported from Ditcheat:

Paul Nicholls yesterday predicted that it will take a monumental
performance from Denman or any other horse to prevent Kauto Star
winning a third Gold Cup, and sealing his place in the pantheon of
jumping legends.

'Kauto Star is going to Cheltenham in the form of his life,' he said.

'What he did at Kempton in the King George was awesome and
he'll go back to Cheltenham in the best form he's ever been. As far as
his chance is concerned, there don't appear to be any chinks in his
armour – he looks bombproof.

'The faster they go in the Gold Cup, the more it will suit him. I said after the King George that if that race were over three and a quarter miles – the distance of the Gold Cup – and not three, he would have ended up winning it by 56 lengths, not 36.'

Nicholls continued: 'And the ground is not an issue nowadays – it was on the soft side when he won his first two Gold Cups and it was pretty tacky when he put up a career-best on Boxing Day.'

Whereas it was always the plan to take the reigning champion – who is 4-6 with the sponsor Totesport – back to Cheltenham without a prep, Nicholls said Denman's run in the Aon 'has brought him on enormously and put him just where we want him'.

He warned it would be 'foolish to write off Denman' when the two outstanding chasers meet in 22 days' time.

Those words will be music to the ears of the sport's marketing gurus, who are desperate to promote the third round of Kauto v Denman as the biggest head-to-head the sport has seen in the last 50 years.

Nicholls said there was no reason why March 19 should be the last time the two chasers clash. 'If we don't overrace them, there's no reason why they can't return again next year.'

Nicholls predicted this year's third favourite Imperial Commander – cut to 10-1 (from 12) by Stan James yesterday – would be the biggest stumbling block to his winning a fifth Gold Cup, following See More Business (1999), Kauto Star in 2007 and last year, and Denman in 2008.

Two weeks before Cheltenham, Steve Dennis visited Manor Farm Stables and caught up with Clifford Baker to talk about Baker's career and the role Kauto Star has played in his life:

Here's a quiz question for you: name the only man to ride the winners of five Gold Cups. Pat Taaffe? No. Aubrey Brabazon? Tommy Carberry? Fred Winter? No. Search the record books and you'll search in vain.

Clifford Baker, a quiet, undemonstrative man, smiles almost shyly as he recites the names of Charter Party, See More Business, Kauto Star and Denman. In just over two weeks' time he may well have stretched his sequence to six, what with Gold Cup winners being

Friendly rivalry: Paul Nicholls with
Kauto Star (left) and Denman

fairly common currency at Paul Nicholls' yard where Baker is head
man, the solid centre around which everything revolves.

Baker is the epitome of a team player, and he stresses that when
Cheltenham comes round on its annual orbit it becomes less about
individuals and all about the team. Baker is as close as anyone to the
great Kauto Star, closer even than Nicholls, as close as the horse's
groom Nick Child, but Cheltenham is no time to play favourites.

'It's not about him winning Gold Cups, but about one of our
horses winning Gold Cups,' he says. 'It's the whole thing, not just
him, and I want all of it. That's the most important thing. We're
very competitive and we gear the whole season round Cheltenham.
When you've got the horses we've got you're always thinking about
Cheltenham.'

Baker, who will be 50 this year, has spent his entire career
thinking about Cheltenham. He's had just two employers in his

life, remarkable enough given the modern tendency to wander, but when those guv'nors have been David Nicholson and Nicholls the natural reaction is to stay put. Now he works just a couple of miles from where he grew up, from where his interest in horses sprang.

'I fell into horses rather than choosing them by choice,' he says. 'When I was young I was a mad footballer, played up front and scored goals, but one day I went over on my ankle and injured it.

'I went to the doctor, he sent me to a specialist, and he told me I'd have to wear a caliper for six months. I was only ten, so it was a big drawback, a big inconvenience. The specialist said that a couple of things that would help the healing process were swimming and horseriding. And I didn't like swimming.'

Baker exchanged his football boots for riding boots and started spending his spare time at the riding school down the road. Swiftly beguiled by his new interest, he moved through the stages of riding someone else's ponies, riding his own pony, going out with the local hunt. And one day a young man has to decide what to do with his life. Baker went to see the local bookmaker.

'I wanted to be a jockey,' says Baker. 'But Dad was a farmer and my family had no connections with racing, knew nothing about it. These days you'd find it all on the internet, but not in the mid-1970s. So we went to the local bookie and asked for the addresses of half a dozen jump trainers, and we wrote to them. We didn't know any other way of doing it.'

The bookie did Baker proud. He suggested writing to Frenchie Nicholson because of his talent for bringing through young jockeys, so the letter was sent and the reply came that Baker should contact Frenchie's son David. Another letter went off and an interview followed, as did a job.

Baker started at the bottom, paid his dues and worked his way through the ranks. Three weeks before Charter Party won the 1988 Gold Cup he took over as head lad, his dreams of being a jockey unsentimentally put aside years earlier. 'I had 17 rides and one winner, on a horse called Kevin Evans for Jenny Pitman,' he says. 'It wasn't for me, though, I knew I wasn't good enough to make it as a jockey.'

He had found his niche anyway. Trainers need a head man in whom they can place implicit trust, and Baker settled into that role as though he'd been born for it. Nicholson was champion trainer twice with Baker at his right hand, in the days of Viking Flagship, Barton Bank, Waterloo Boy and Mysilv, and Baker stayed there 19 years.

'Not everybody got on that well with the Duke, but I always did, there were never any cross words,' he says. 'But it was time to move on. I knew Paul Barber – everyone does round here – and the area was home to me anyway. There were 40 horses when I arrived in the summer of 1996, and I'd never have dreamed that we'd have what we have here now. It was the best move I've ever made – mind you, I've only made two.'

Head man is a relatively anonymous position, there being too much work to do at home to waste time gadding off to racecourses or gassing to the media. It is fair to say that Nicholls would not have occupied the heights he has reached, and kept, without the unassuming Baker pulling the strings; horses come and go but men you can trust are worth their weight in gold, in Gold Cups.

See More Business was only a youngster when Baker arrived in the yard, but he rode him in the course of his duties as he had Charter Party, as he does Denman. Kauto Star is slightly different, as Baker rides him the vast majority of the time.

Six-year-old Charlotte – the youngest of Baker's three children – 'absolutely adores' Kauto Star, has all the badges, rosettes, a scarf, and goes to the same school as Nicholls' daughter Megan, the same as Barber's grandchildren. It's a proper school; on Gold Cup day the children are allowed to watch the big race on television. Baker will be at Cheltenham that day, his only visit of the week as the other three days will be spent at Ditcheat, keeping his head, keeping a lid on all the excitement, keeping the show on the road.

'The pressure doesn't get to me too much,' he says. 'I take it all in my stride. If I start getting wound up then the staff will get wound up, then the horses, and it's just not worth it.

'I'm up at 5.30 and in just before six to feed the 82 horses we have in the main yard, and I do the hay for the morning, things like that, which takes around an hour.

'Then Paul comes in and we run through the list of what every horse is going to do exercise-wise. First lot goes out at 8am – I don't always ride first lot, maybe there's a bit of schooling to be done – and then I go out on Kauto second lot.

WELL, ONE OF US HAS TO LET GO — RACE YOU FOR IT !!

Denman and Kauto Star tussle over the Cheltenham Gold Cup – as imagined by artist Martin Alford

'Third lot I'm back in the yard, sorting out problems from the day before, any cuts and bruises. I give the horses their lunch, head home for mine, and I'm back here at 2.45pm for evening stables. I check every horse, make sure everything is going smoothly and that all the horses are all right.'

He has no favourites in the yard, says that he doesn't get attached to any of the horses, but the conversation swings back to Kauto Star and a certain animation is easy to detect. 'It's my fifth season riding him, at the beginning he was just one I dropped in and rode.

'He's still as sharp now as he was then. He may have mellowed a tiny bit but he hasn't really changed, and I think that's why he's as good as he is.

'His first Gold Cup was one of my best festivals, because we had Denman winning as well and we knew they'd both be back the following year. Charter Party and See More Business were gallopers, but this horse has won two Tingle Creeks, four King Georges on the trot and the last one was a mindblowing performance – no big race should be won like that.

'I don't see why he can't win another King George . . . but you never know. One thing I do know is that I'll never see another as good as him.'

And then he says he's a lucky man to sit on four Gold Cup winners, to work with brilliant horses, to work with a great team.

If you ask me, they're the lucky ones.

'The decider – Kauto v Denman III' was how the Racing Post *splashed on Gold Cup day 2010, but it was a horse whom Paul Nicholls had earlier named as the main stumbling block to the chasing crown*

Racegoers at Cheltenham sport Kauto Star scarves, 19 March 2010

CHELTENHAM, 19 March 2010			
Totesport Cheltenham Gold Cup Chase		3m2½f	
1	Imperial Commander	7-1	P Brennan
2	Denman	4-1	AP McCoy
3	Mon Mome	50-1	A Coleman
F	Kauto Star	8-11f	R Walsh
11 ran 7l, 23l			

returning to Ditcheat – Imperial Commander – who took the honours. Graham Dench reported:

Ruby Walsh is met by reporters after Kauto Star's fall in the Cheltenham Gold Cup, 19 March 2010

Dreams of Kauto Star winning a third Gold Cup came to an abrupt end when he fell four fences out. In truth they had all but evaporated much earlier.

Kauto Star's great rival Denman fared much better with an honourable seven-length second, having looked the winner for much of the way. He will now be aimed at next year's John Smith's Grand National – at least he will if co-owner Harry Findlay has his way.

Essentially a brilliant jumper, though always prone to the occasional aberration, Kauto Star had survived a shocking mistake at the eighth, where Ruby Walsh had done well to stay on board. He was still on the heels of the winner when he came down, but Walsh had been riding with increasing urgency.

Walsh, who remounted Kauto Star and hacked him back, said: 'That's racing. It's disappointing, but these things happen. It's steeplechasing and the fences are there to be jumped. But he's all right, I'm all right, and there will be another day.

'He travelled beautifully until the first mistake, but it was a bad mistake and obviously had an effect on him. After that I could not get a position or on an even keel. After a mistake like that you are fighting a lost cause. It's not as simple as turning up and collecting the prize money.'

The following day Nicholls said that his two stars were fine when they arrived back home, as Tom O'Ryan reported:

Defeated they may have been, but Ditcheat's 'big two' Kauto Star and Denman were far from deflated yesterday as they relaxed back in familiar surroundings, side-by-side, at Paul Nicholls' Manor Farm yard.

Kauto Star, who suffered a rare fall four from home in his bid to win the Cheltenham Gold Cup for a third time, and Denman, who finished a courageous runner-up to Imperial Commander in Friday's showpiece event, both returned to their Somerset base that night.

'They're both fine,' reported Nicholls yesterday. 'Kauto is a little bit stiff and sore after his fall, as you'd expect, but he's bright in himself, as is Denman, who has come out of his race really well. The pair of them are grand, fit and well, and they live to fight another day.'

That day may be a while in coming. Nicholls has yet to sit down to discuss the future with the horses' owners, but he said: 'I think it's very unlikely either of them will run again this season.

'Next season, I would love to think that Denman could go back and win a third Hennessy, and that Kauto could win another King George; they would be their targets at the end of the year.'

It was time for another summer of rest and reflection after a gruelling season, and it was in July that Kauto Star and Denman both returned after their breaks. Ben Newton reported:

Kauto Star and Denman have returned to training 'both looking a picture' after their summer break, according to trainer Paul Nicholls

– but plans are still up in the air over where they will reappear.

Jump racing's pair of celebrities spent ten weeks together in a field adjacent to Nicholls' home at Highbridge Farm, near Ditcheat.

For company, they had regular summer companions Big Buck's and Master Minded, and were joined by What A Friend and Tataniano, both Grade 1 winners last season.

Nicholls said: 'Kauto and Denman both enjoyed themselves out in the field and have come back in looking in wonderful condition.

'Master Minded and What A Friend left the others a fortnight early as they were among a batch who went off for a breathing operation.'

He stressed that early targets for Kauto Star are still up for discussion. 'All roads lead to Kempton on Boxing Day again as far as Kauto is concerned, and I am due to meet Clive shortly to plan where we start off,' he said.

'After the horrible fall Kauto had in the Gold Cup, it's always at the back of my mind that it may have left a mental scar on him and he might go out and remember it. But he's old enough and wise enough to forget it, hopefully.

'It was so bad that for a fortnight after Cheltenham he couldn't put his head to the ground. But he schooled fine before we turned him out, so he should be okay.'

It was at Nicholls' annual owners' open day that the champion trainer stated that Kauto Star would probably head to Down Royal for his seasonal return.

Another star was on the horizon, though, as Nicholls spoke about the challenge posed by Long Run, who had run third in the RSA Chase. Ben Newton reported:

Kauto Star fans will have to wait until Boxing Day to see the chasing legend back in action in Britain after Paul Nicholls revealed yesterday he is likely to sidestep a rematch with Imperial Commander in the Betfair Chase and head to Ireland on November 6 for his first run of the season.

Kauto Star has landed three of the last four runnings of Haydock's Grade 1 chase, scraping home by a nose from the subsequent Gold Cup winner 12 months ago, but Nicholls said:

'I'm sure Nigel [Twiston-Davies] will have Imperial Commander absolutely spot-on for the Betfair, and so to beat him again at Haydock Kauto Star would need to be at the top of his game. But I don't want him at peak fitness for that race; I want to have him spot-on for Boxing Day, when it would be fantastic for everyone if he could win the King George for the fifth time. It's for that reason that we are likely to go to Down Royal for the JNWine. com Champion Chase, a race he won in 2008 and one which fits in perfectly, as it then gives us seven weeks to get him spot-on for the King George.'

He added: 'After Down Royal, the plan will be the King George and then, all being well, back to Cheltenham for his fifth run in the Gold Cup.'

Kauto Star is a best-priced 9-4 with King George sponsor William Hill and Stan James to enter the record books and sit alongside Golden

Ruby Walsh (right) and his wife Gillian visit Kauto Star and Nick Child at Ditcheat

Miller, the last horse to win the same championship chase five years in a row, when he won the Cheltenham Gold Cup from 1932 to '36.

To equal that feat Kauto Star will have to overcome the up-and-coming Long Run, but Nicholls warned: 'While I respect Long Run, he has to improve before his form reaches the level of Kauto, Denman and Imperial Commander. He might do just that, but last season's RSA Chase, where he finished third, was not a vintage renewal in my book, and although he'd earlier won the Feltham in a fast time, our runner, Tchico Polos, who was second favourite, was a blatant non-stayer. Long Run is going to turn out more a two-and-a-half-mile horse, but we'll respect him and anything else that takes us on in the King George.'

Clive Smith said in the run-up to Down Royal that this was likely to be Kauto Star's 'last real season'. Although Kauto posted a 14th

Kauto Star is paraded at Paul Nicholls' owners' open day

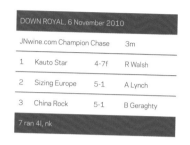

DOWN ROYAL, 6 November 2010		
JNwine.com Champion Chase	3m	
1 Kauto Star	4-7f	R Walsh
2 Sizing Europe	5-1	A Lynch
3 China Rock	5-1	B Geraghty
7 ran 4l, nk		

top-level success in the Champion Chase, the day ended in misery for Ruby Walsh after he sustained a double fracture of his right leg in a later race. Brian Fleming reported:

Paul Nicholls was 'thrilled to bits' after Kauto Star had won the JNwine.com Champion Chase at Down Royal yesterday but said the dual Cheltenham Gold Cup winner would have to recover quickly if he is to line up in the Hennessy Gold Cup in 20 days' time.

The alternative is to wait for the William Hill King George VI Chase on Boxing Day. After registering his second win in Down Royal's biggest race, Kauto Star was unchanged at 7-4 with the sponsors for the Kempton showpiece.

Nicholls said: 'I told Clive Smith that if we are going to run in the Hennessy he'll need to start back in work shortly, so we'll have to see how he is after this, with the travel and everything. I'll know more at the end of next week if Newbury is on for him.'

Kauto Star bounced back from his fall in the Gold Cup with a four-length win over Sizing Europe and China Rock, his 21st career success.

'I left plenty to work on coming here and he beat two decent horses, so I'm thrilled to bits,' Nicholls said. 'He made a mistake in the Gold Cup and paid the price for it, but we have done a lot with his jumping since.'

Stan James left Kauto Star unchanged at 5-1 to win the Gold Cup in March but cut him to 5-4 (from 7-4) to win a fifth King George. He is also 5-4 with Ladbrokes.

Exciting French-bred Long Run was emerging as the latest challenger to Kauto Star, as Graham Dench reported in December:

Robert Waley-Cohen believes his hugely promising five-year-old Long Run can pose a real threat to the history-seeking Kauto Star in the William Hill King George VI Chase, for which he is 5-1 clear second favourite with the sponsors.

Waley-Cohen has the utmost respect for Kauto Star but says he is 'very much hoping to spoil the party' when the ten-year-old bids for an unprecedented fifth successive win in the race on Boxing Day.

Kauto Star is driven home by Ruby Walsh in the Champion Chase at Down Royal, 6 November 2010

Waley-Cohen said: 'Kauto is king and he's an absolute superstar, but we have to try to topple him and Long Run has the greatest potential of any horse I've been involved with.'

Waley-Cohen is encouraged by the relative form the King George principals showed in their youth in France.

'Long Run is the only horse who has ever won the Grade 1 hurdle for three-year-olds and the Grade 1 chase for four-year-olds. I know horses improve at different rates, but in France he was rated 3kg better than Kauto Star was at the same stage. If you look at him it's remarkable that he did what he did over hurdles because he's a big, strong chaser yet he's got real speed. He grew again in the summer and he's come on for his run in the Paddy Power too.'

Paul Nicholls had equally positive news about the King George favourite, who is joint top-priced with William Hill at evens and will be schooled for a second time by stand-in rider Noel Fehily next week.

Nicholls said: 'He hasn't been held up at all by the weather and you saw on Saturday that mine are in great form. Clifford says he's feeling as good as ever. I'd say he's looking as good as ever too.'

Kauto Star walks through Ditcheat on a crisp December morning

The race was postponed until the middle of January after snow affected large parts of Britain over Christmas.

When the race was eventually run a bumper crowd was left astonished as it appeared they had witnessed the ending of one era and the dawning of another after Long Run gave Nicky Henderson a first King George VI Chase and Kauto Star a 19-length beating into third. Graham Dench reported:

Hopes of Kauto Star winning a record fifth consecutive King George started to fade with the best part of a mile to go, but retirement is by no means a foregone conclusion after he finished an honourable third.

The 15,000 crowd, many of them sporting Kauto Star scarves and nearly all willing him to win, were left wondering if age might have caught up with him, but neither Paul Nicholls nor Clive Smith was in any hurry to call time on his career.

Unless something emerges when he is checked out at home, Nicholls sees no reason why he should not return to Cheltenham in March to bid for a third Totesport Gold Cup.

Some bookmakers have virtually written him off, and he is as big as 12-1 for the Gold Cup with yesterday's sponsor William Hill. Totesport quote 10-1.

KEMPTON, 15 January 2011		
William Hill King George VI Chase	3m	
1 Long Run	9-2	Mr S Waley-Cohen
2 Riverside Theatre	10-1	B Geraghty
3 Kauto Star	4-7f	AP McCoy
9 ran 12l, 7l		

Kauto Star jumps the last at Kempton but Long Run (centre) and Riverside Theatre (left) have his measure in the King George VI Chase, 15 January 2011

Nicholls said: 'I'll have a talk with Clive, but if he's sound and well there is no reason why he can't run in the Gold Cup. Cheltenham will suit him better than Kempton does now, as he's just that bit slower. He looked like he'd lost half a yard around here at the age of 11.

'There wasn't any stage at which I thought he'd win. I was never happy but I have no excuse, as everything had gone right with him.

'Although Ruby and I were both happy with him at Down Royal, age might be catching up with him. I feel as if I've let everyone down, but he's been here five times and won four. We'll get him home and see if we can come up with an explanation.'

Smith proffered a possible explanation for Kauto Star's unusually flat display when he said: 'Nick Child, his lad, said that when he went into the box this morning Kauto wasn't whizzing around like he usually is, so maybe he just wasn't feeling so great.

'It might be the end of an era, but he's been a wonderful horse and hopefully still is. Everyone wanted to see history made, but nobody let anyone down. Tony [McCoy] came in and said sorry, but I told him not to worry about it. We'll see how he is, but if there is any sign of ageing we'll call it a day.'

Reflecting on a stellar career that has yielded 21 victories, 17 since he arrived from France in 2004 and 14 at Grade 1 level, Smith

singled out Kauto Star's 36-length victory in 2009 as the pick of the four King George wins. He said: 'I treasure him for what he's done, and I admire and respect him so much. Nothing's changed about how good he is. You definitely mustn't write him off.'

McCoy could not explain the disappointing effort and was at a loss to see what he might have done differently.

He said: 'I came back in and told Paul someone else would have to say what I did wrong, because I couldn't tell him.

'Ruby told me to keep squeezing him, and I was doing that, but halfway around the bottom bend I thought I should be picking up more than I was doing. He missed the second-last but only because I was drilling him. It was a tired mistake.

'He might not be as quick as he used to be, but I thought he would have picked up more than he did. Even though he's won four King Georges, he's also won two Gold Cups – any horse that wins the Gold Cup has to be an out-and-out stayer.'

The following day Smith and Nicholls re-emphasised their determination to race on and try for a third Gold Cup, as Bruce Jackson reported:

Kauto Star is not for retiring and is up to the challenge of winning a third Gold Cup in March.

That was the message from owner Clive Smith and champion trainer Paul Nicholls after the 11-year-old's attempt to win the King George VI Chase for a record fifth time came up short when he finished third behind Long Run and Riverside Theatre at Kempton on Saturday.

Nicholls revealed yesterday that Kauto Star had bled slightly when he got back home on Saturday evening but the trainer was not using that as an excuse for defeat, believing it may have been caused by making a mistake at the second-last fence when he was trailing Long Run.

Kauto Star will have a short break to recover before being prepared for Cheltenham – he is as big as 12-1 for the Totesport-sponsored Gold Cup with Stan James and William Hill – and a defiant Nicholls said yesterday: 'It's not over yet. I'm sure he will be back winning again. Cheltenham is a different day, different track and different ground, so it could be a different story.

Tony McCoy's expression tells the story after Kauto Star's defeat at Kempton

'He will go for the Gold Cup if we are happy with him. Talk about retirement is premature. He doesn't show any signs of ageing at home and has already won a Grade 1 this season.

'I would love to go back and win the Down Royal race [JNwine. com Champion Chase] for a third time, but that's a long way off.'

After talking with Nicholls on Sunday morning, Smith said: 'We came to the conclusion that there is plenty of life in him still and we think he had an off-day.

'We always have the best interest of the horse at heart and we would have a serious think about retirement if he did it again, but he isn't showing us he is ready to retire.'

Nicholls campaigned 1999 Gold Cup winner See More Business to finish third behind Best Mate as a 12-year-old and then saddled him in the race a year later.

He said: 'I was watching Match of the Day this morning and they were saying how when footballers get over 30 people write them off. Kauto is only 11, not 13. He's run a cracking race and I'm happy with the way he is. He's in great shape this morning.'

Reflecting on the race, Nicholls added: 'He would have been a good second if he had jumped the second-last. He has still run a cracking race and done amazingly well to finish third, although he was very tired after the last.

'It just didn't happen for him yesterday and he was beaten by a younger pair of legs. On the second circuit, when he normally wings away, he made three or four jumps that didn't gain him the advantage it has in the past and let him bound away out of the back straight.'

Although Ruby Walsh missed the King George, the Irishman joined Kauto's connections in insisting that the two-time Gold Cup winner should not be written off. Brian Fleming reported:

Ruby Walsh said yesterday that it would be premature to write off Kauto Star based on his performance at Kempton on Saturday, adding that he thought the brilliant chaser 'just didn't spark' on the day.

Walsh, who has partnered Kauto Star to victory 15 times from 22 attempts during his career, said yesterday: 'It was disappointing he didn't win a fifth King George, but they are not machines and you can't just turn them on and off.

'He often had better days in the past but he had a few off days in the past too, so you can't write him off on just one day. He just didn't spark and as we all know humans have some off days too. As Paul said this morning, AP said had he jumped the second- last well he would have been a good second. It's a long way to Cheltenham for him and Denman and all the other contenders and time will tell a lot.'

Walsh was lavish in his praise for the Nicky Henderson-trained winner and rider Sam Waley-Cohen.

He said: 'Long Run was very good on the day and Sam gave him a great ride. The game needs families like the Waley-Cohens and Sam doesn't just turn up on the day. He does his homework well, knows the form, and is extremely fit for an amateur, so hats off to him.'

Kauto Star spent the next couple of weeks on the easy list after he bled during the race and was later found to be suffering from inflammation and a low-grade infection, for which he was given a course of antibiotics before beginning his Cheltenham preparations.

The day before the Gold Cup Clive Smith said: 'It's a big thing to ask at 11 maybe, but Paul says he is in as good shape as he was for the last Gold Cup.

'He was okay before the King George and something came to light after the race. Clifford Baker, who rides him every day, says he is in very good order and I think he is the best judge of all.

'I have to be optimistic. There are certain statistics, like Long Run having to become the first of his age since Mill House in 1963 to win the Gold Cup, and the other is that ten-year-olds and upwards don't have a very good record. There are three Gold Cup winners, one is ten and two 11.'

Win or lose, Smith said this might not be Kauto Star's last run. He added: 'You don't get too many chances to have a horse like this. Desert Orchid won his last King George aged 11. I think he can certainly race throughout this year. It would be nice to send him out on a high but we are not going to make any quick decisions.'

The Gold Cup turned into a sensational race:

In one of the greatest runnings of the Cheltenham Gold Cup Long Run dethroned Denman and Kauto Star to offer a hint that the guard was changing at the top of steeplechasing. The 'old' guard were brushed aside by the six-year-old upstart in a track record time.

Paul Nicholls said afterwards of his pair, who finished second and third: 'I wasn't expecting very much today but both Denman and Kauto were awesome.

'I thought going to the second-last we might have a chance, but the younger legs of Long Run were just too much for them.

'Long Run was the best horse in the race but mine have run absolutely blinding races. They have given their all and I'm immensely proud of them. What I've got to do now is find one to tackle Long Run. It won't be easy.'

Looking to the future, Nicholls refused to rush into any snap decisions about whether the two veterans will race again.

He said: 'I'm not going to make any quick decisions although I've always felt Kauto might be half-suited by going to Punchestown.

'For Denman there's not a lot left this season as he has to go left-handed and won't be going to Aintree. On that sort of form, though, there's no reason why he shouldn't run in another Hennessy.

'They won't be abused and if they show any sign that they aren't capable of running well again they won't run. However, they've run well today and have shown we made the right call by running them.'

Smith added: 'He's been a wonderful horse. I'm not saying that in the past tense, or that he's definitely finished, but he's probably finished in Gold Cups.

'He's been terrific, such a lovely, tough, game horse. It was an extraordinary race and very emotional. We'll think about the future but he certainly loves racing and being in training.'

Ruby Walsh added: 'What can you say about any horse who has run as well as he has? He's run terrific and fair play to Paul Nicholls and his team for getting him here for five Gold Cups.

'He ran a cracking race, it's just that he is 11 now and the overdrive just isn't there any more.'

Smith later hinted that a trip to Punchestown could be on the agenda if retirement is shelved, a plan which was confirmed the following month.

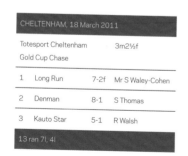

CHELTENHAM, 18 March 2011			
Totesport Cheltenham Gold Cup Chase		3m2½f	
1	Long Run	7-2f	Mr S Waley-Cohen
2	Denman	8-1	S Thomas
3	Kauto Star	5-1	R Walsh
13 ran 7l, 4l			

Smith said: 'If he comes out of next week's race well, comes back after a good summer and feels good on the gallops, then we'll go on with him – if he's not enjoying it, he'll be retired.

'He came out of the Gold Cup in very good order and we decided to miss Sandown because the ground would have been very firm. We were glad we didn't risk him there. Hopefully the ground at Punchestown will be watered well and he can run a good race.'

It all went horribly wrong at Punchestown, as Lee Mottershead reported:

The moment Kauto Star was pulled up by Ruby Walsh after the 13th fence of yesterday's Punchestown Guinness Gold Cup was greeted with both sadness and relief.

The sadness was that an all-time jumping great should be seen performing so far below his once imperious best. The relief came from the knowledge that, by being removed from the race, he would return home safe.

The question now facing connections is not whether Kauto Star remains capable of competing with distinction, for his Cheltenham Gold Cup third showed that he undoubtedly can.

The brutal question Paul Nicholls and Clive Smith will ask themselves is whether, in the worthy desire to see him go out on a high, they can risk an exceptional story coming to a more ignominious end.

After the lengthy debrief that followed Kauto Star's listless display, Nicholls and Smith agreed a line. They said the winner of two Cheltenham Gold Cups and four King George VI Chases would enjoy a summer at grass with Denman, before both are prepared for another season.

However, it became immediately obvious that, while the trainer's inclination was to wait and see, the owner's desire was to play safe.

Although making clear that 'there is definitely no decision yet', Smith could not hide his deeper feelings.

'There might be some spark left, but I don't want to squeeze the last drop out of him,' he said.

'He has had a fantastic career and I love him to bits. People would love to see him win more races but the old body wears out.

PUNCHESTOWN, 4 May 2011			
Punchestown Guinness Gold Cup Chase		3m1f	
1	Follow The Plan	20-1	T Doyle
2	Vic Venturi	40-1	B Geraghty
3	Rare Bob	20-1	P Carberry
PU	Kauto Star	10-11f	R Walsh
8 ran 11l, 4½l			

Previous spread: Long Run leads
Denman and Kauto Star over the final
fence in the Cheltenham Gold Cup,
18 March 2011

Right: A disconsolate Ruby Walsh
hacks back on Kauto Star after pulling
him up at Punchestown, 4 May 2011

I'm willing to see what he is like after a summer out at grass and then we'll assess things in October. Paul is right in what he has said, but I would like to see him rest up, go into a paddock and retire.'

Nicholls, whose affection for Kauto Star has never been hidden, had earlier told partner Georgie Browne that he did not care where his once invincible champion finished 'as long as he comes back safe and sound'.

Kauto Star did, but the writing was on the wall with a circuit to go. 'He jumped very well but was never really on the bridle,' said Walsh, whose first serious urgings came a mile from home. They achieved nothing. Where once everything was simple for Kauto Star, it was hard work yesterday.

'This job would be a lot easier if horses could talk,' said Nicholls. 'It's the end of the season and he just hasn't fired, but even Nacarat ran well below form.

'He will be a long time retired, so I won't make any rash decisions. I suspect we'll give him a nice holiday and bring him back in the autumn. Then if he runs like that again it is obvious what we'll do.'

Kauto Star's career has outshone those of almost all the horses who have gone before him and we may never see his like again. We may also never see him race again. Yesterday, however, was not the time for decisions.

It was left to Alastair Down to sum up the despondent mood felt by many in the sport:

A much-loved chasing legend finds himself at a crossroads in the twilight of his career after Kauto Star was pulled up in the Guinness Gold Cup at Punchestown, sparking a debate over whether the old trouper should now be earmarked for field rather than fray.

He looked a touch dry in his coat and end-of-termish in the paddock beforehand and as far as nine fences from home Ruby Walsh, who can mask the fact a horse is not travelling better than anyone, was to my eye giving out those little signals that he was not happy with how his old ally was going.

In fact he was the first beat and Ruby pulled him up with four fences still to jump. Immediately there were those to be heard saying we had seen the last of Kauto Star in action.

Before people get aerated and hot under the collar it should be remembered that the final decision will be taken by the horse's close connections who love this horse every bit as much if not more than the general public and have served him brilliantly down the years.

Clive Smith seems minded to call it a day but expressed himself more than happy to listen to those who think the horse deserves another chance to prove he can hack it at the top level.

And Paul Nicholls certainly seems in no mood to rush to judgement. He was at pains to point out that yesterday's race came at the end of a long season and that it was both premature and unfair to judge his old warrior on this run alone.

It is actually a very hard call and a more complex decision than it would first appear. Racehorses are not electric toys that can be switched off and put away in a cupboard. Nor are they kids' ponies happy to do no more than eat their heads off in some backwater field. Plenty of retired racehorses simply don't take to the easy life and there was an almost plaintive note in Nicholls' voice when, in relation to the horse being retired, he asked: 'What would you do with him?'

Both Nicholls and Smith were in accord that one more lacklustre run from Kauto Star would result in him being retired. And I think the decision-making process is made more difficult when you stop and ask yourself which races next year would Kauto Star, who will turn 12 in mid-season, have a real chance of winning.

If he still held his King George title you could have that as his principal target, but Long Run took that off him en route to Gold Cup glory and even diehard Kauto Star fans could not, hand on heart, expect him to be a force in terms of winning at Cheltenham in March.

But of course he didn't have to win the Gold Cup six weeks ago to play the most glorious part in what was surely one of the greatest staying chases of all time.

We can all rest assured that there is no chance whatsoever of us having to watch Kauto Star in some sad decline, getting chinned by lesser animals he would have picked up and carried in his prime.

What Nicholls, Smith and Clifford Baker have to decide is exactly what is best for the horse and we can trust them to do that.

Perhaps the intensity of the discussion about his future was yet another reminder of what we owe this horse and the magnificence of his contribution to all our days in recent years.

He could very easily come back and win another James Nicholson at Down Royal in November and that perhaps would afford everyone a winning note on which to bow out. He could then spend the rest of the season putting the youngsters through their paces at Ditcheat.

In all honesty, his fabulous Gold Cup third last month told us that while the fires still burn they no longer do so with the fearsome ferocity of old.

Now it is about orchestrating his farewell and we can leave that to those who have husbanded him in mind and body so outstandingly through the long harvest of the seasons.

He is a Ditcheat animal. Leave them to do right by him.

7

Resurrection

*AFTER A SUMMER break Kauto Star was back in training for an
eighth British campaign, and Paul Nicholls was happy to write off
Punchestown as a one-off and see if his superstar was ready for the
challenges that lay ahead.*

*Ben Newton reported from the champion trainer's open day in
September:*

The future for Kauto Star is likely to be decided at Haydock
on November 19 after the chasing legend makes his probable
reappearance in the Betfair Chase.

Talk of retirement was firmly off the agenda yesterday when
Britain's best-loved chaser headed a galaxy of stars who were
paraded at Paul Nicholls' annual owners' open day.

The pressure was on for connections to call it a day with the dual
Gold Cup winner following his lacklustre display when pulled up in
the Guinness Gold Cup at Punchestown in May, easily his poorest
effort in a stellar 38-race career that has netted a record £2.16
million in prize money.

Nicholls said: 'Kauto came out of his third place in the Gold Cup
so well that it made his Punchestown run such a mystery. On the
balance of his form last season he's not exactly a back-number yet
and is still capable of producing high-class form over fences, so he
deserves the chance to show Punchestown was a one-off. After all,
most of the Gold Cup horses who ran again subsequently performed
below their best.

'The decision whether or not he carries on rests with Clive, who is
very keen to see him run again. Nothing is set in stone, but we'll keep
everyone informed and the favoured option is the Betfair Chase,
which he won in 2006, 2007 and 2009. After that we can take a
view whether to carry on. Looking at him you wouldn't say he's had
enough and he's in grand order.'

To those who feel connections should draw stumps now, Nicholls
added: 'We are not going to be greedy, we'll do what's best for the
horse. If he gives the slightest indication he's had enough, that'll be
it.'

Kauto Star (right) has a racecourse gallop with Big Buck's at Exeter

The Betfair Chase was being billed as D-day for Kauto's future and retirement after the race was a real option, as David Milnes reported:

Kauto Star's future hinges on how he performs on his seasonal return in the Betfair Chase at Haydock this month, owner Clive Smith underlined yesterday.

The 11-year-old dual Cheltenham Gold Cup winner is one of 19 entries for the Grade 1 on November 19, which he has won three times, along with last season's Gold Cup winner Long Run.

Kauto Star is on a comeback mission after flopping at Punchestown in May, but he went well in a racecourse gallop at Exeter on Tuesday.

Smith said: 'It looks as though this year's Betfair Chase is going to be a very good race and I'm looking forward to seeing Kauto Star return to Haydock.

'Everything will come out regarding his future after Haydock. He could be retired instantly or he might be around for another go at the Gold Cup. There are so many factors and he isn't the oldest horse in training. See More Business was third in the Gold Cup as a 12-year-old and Kauto Star is in great shape.'

Smith added: 'He certainly doesn't have to win the Betfair Chase to race on. If he is beaten by 20 lengths and looks fed up, we'll call it a day, but if he is right there with them and is beaten by four or five lengths it could show that he is still in fine fettle.'

Nicholls said that Kauto was 'ready to run for his life', and he did just do that as he brought the house down for an emotional victory that thrilled everyone at Haydock Park. Tom O'Ryan reported:

Kauto Star (right) defeats Long Run (left) and Weird Al in the Betfair Chase at Haydock, 19 November 2011

Haydock erupted just after 3.12pm yesterday.

In scenes of jubilation and undiluted celebration among racegoers seldom witnessed outside of Cheltenham and Aintree, one of the greatest heavyweight chasers of this or any other generation was treated to the sort of emotional reception which stirs the heart, quickens the pulse and provides a sharp reminder of why battle-hardened stars of the jumping game command so much affection and admiration.

Kauto Star may be in the autumn of his career, but he shone like a primetime performer when winning his fourth Betfair Chase, comprehensively turning the tables on Long Run, who had beaten him into third in last season's Cheltenham Gold Cup.

Cheered in the parade ring, cheered going down and cheered coming back, the ultra-popular 11-year-old jumped like the proverbial stag for Ruby Walsh.

It was stirring stuff. After leading throughout, he first shrugged off the attentions of Time For Rupert and then Diamond Harry before he hit overdrive in the home straight.

Come the line, by which time the roar from the stands was deafening, he had put eight lengths between himself and Long Run, with Charlie Hall Chase winner Weird Al a further two lengths back in third.

Remarkably, it was his 15th Grade 1 victory and was achieved in front of a near 11,000-strong crowd – Haydock's biggest attendance for a jumps meeting in five years.

'This is my proudest-ever moment,' declared Paul Nicholls, who appeared close to tears at times among the throng in the unsaddling enclosure when 'Hip, hip, hooray' rang out around the packed crowd.

'To do what he's done at the age of 11 and beat a Gold Cup winner is phenomenal . . . awesome . . . unbelievable. Him and Ruby are made for each other. We left no stone unturned coming into this race. This was his Gold Cup.'

Nicholls had a message for those who had felt it was time for Kauto Star to be retired. 'I think they should eat their words and apologise. I took some flak about running him today, but I told everyone he'd never been better.

HAYDOCK, 19 November 2011			
Betfair Chase		3m	
1	Kauto Star	6-1	R Walsh
2	Long Run	6-5f	Mr S Waley-Cohen
3	Weird Al	7-1	T Murphy
6 ran 8l, 2l			

'I think the world of this horse and I wouldn't carry on with him if I didn't think he was capable of doing himself justice.

'At home he was looking well and was going well and I came here sure he'd run well. I've always wanted to make the running with him and I felt this was the day to do it.'

Kauto Star, who has now won 22 races, was cut to 4-1 (from 16) for the King George VI Chase with sponsors William Hill, but Nicholls would not be drawn on whether that Kempton prize, which Kauto Star has already won a remarkable four times, would again figure on his Christmas agenda.

'I haven't looked beyond today. Let's get him home, make sure he's sound in the morning and then sit down and talk about it.'

Owner Clive Smith is, however, already looking forward to his now familiar Kempton pilgrimage.

He said: 'It's only five weeks away and he's obviously very well in himself, so hopefully we'll be there.'

Smith, also the owner of the Nicholls-trained Master Minded, winner of Ascot's Amlin Chase, was overjoyed at Kauto Star's return to former glories, especially after he had pulled up at Punchestown in May.

He added: 'Today is brilliant and to think where we were at Punchestown. He really is an amazing horse.'

Walsh would agree with that. Having provided Kauto Star with a ride of pure poetry, the jockey was beaming from ear to ear on his way back to the winner's circle as the cheers rang out.

'What a horse he is. He was enjoying himself up front. I could hear Sam [Waley-Cohen] on Long Run slapping and roaring behind him down the back straight, so I knew he must be in some trouble.

'I felt I'd gone a good gallop, but if my lad had stopped to a trot after the last, I would have puked! It's wonderful to be here.'

As Kauto Star was led several times around the parade ring Nicholls looked on in pure admiration.

'It's not relief that I feel,' he said, 'It's pride. I am proud of him.'

He wasn't on his own.

Alastair Down was there on a day when another momentous chapter was written into jumping's rich history:

Another thousand years will never empty jump racing's treasure chest of the remarkable and at Haydock yesterday Kauto Star, ageing yet rampant, made the stiffest of upper lips succumb to the trembles with a victory over Long Run that has to figure on any list of the great chasing performances.

It is now seven years less a month since Kauto Star made his British debut at Newbury and the harvest of the seasons has been bounteous indeed, with two Tingle Creeks, four consecutive King George wins and the first ever regaining of a Gold Cup crown. But yesterday he scaled a summit of a different nature because, for all the warm receptions I have seen him return to at Kempton and Cheltenham, nothing before has matched the acclaim and adoration that built feverishly from the third-last and never ceased until long after he stood steaming and simply superb in the winner's enclosure with the wag's cry of 'Bring on Frankel' ringing in his ears.

It was back in March 2009 that he last won at Cheltenham. There have been two usurpers of his slipping crown since then and here he was conceding five years to Long Run, who had slammed him by 19 lengths in last season's King George and then 11 in the Gold Cup in March.

After he was pulled up at Punchestown at the end of last season the instant judges and angle-seekers who love nothing more than rushing to judgement were sharpening their stilettos and calling for his retirement.

Paul Nicholls was having none of it, begging all with the ears to hear that one day at the buckle-end of term meant nothing, and he took his warrior home to Somerset for rest and recuperation.

Nicholls has been insisting for weeks he had Kauto Star in terrific nick and from flagfall, almost like a declaration of war, Ruby Walsh took the battle to the enemy by setting off in front.

I first fell for Kauto Star the day he was defeated by Denman in the Gold Cup because, despite he and Ruby never hitting a rhythm over his fences, the horse fought on to the bitter end. It was the day it hit home that Kauto Star's class was welded and melded with courage.

Here Kauto and Ruby were in rhythm as one, like some long-established double act who know each other inside out and have a peerless mutual sense of timing. They were a sight to behold because

Paul Nicholls greets Kauto Star after the emotional success at Haydock, 19 November 2011

I am not sure I have ever seen Kauto so good over his fences and as they came towards the end of the back straight – with Long Run already having put in three sloppy jumps – the stands caught that unmistakable whiff on the wind that the leader might just not be for catching.

Be in no doubt as to the depth of desire in this Haydock crowd for Kauto Star to win. The course was awash with scarves in his colours from the moment the doors opened and many among his supporters must have made the journey hoping for victory but also wanting to be on hand just in case this blazing beacon was going to illuminate the racecourse for the last time.

A great phalanx in Kauto's colours roared and applauded Ruby and their hero as they trooped round the top of the paddock and out towards the fray. And by the time Kauto Star was leading them up the home straight the disciples had been joined in their roaring by every other person on course except blood relations of the other runners.

He momentarily looked tired after jumping the second-last, but the power of Ruby's legs drew another rally from him. Amid brewing tumult they were brilliant at the last before powering away to win by eight lengths and my spine must have been just one of thousands down which happy shivers were coursing.

Haydock hit delirium. Something primal lurks deep in the staying chaser and it has the power to grip the soul and raise us high. It manifests itself in exultant roars, caught throats, tears and laughter. Just occasionally at moments such as this it is utterly contagious and the momentum of celebration builds, climbs and takes flight until everyone is caught up in the euphoria of the moment.

Never outside Cheltenham have I seen a horse strike such a deep and joyous chord with the crowd – now his crowd. This truly was the day when the very stones cried out.

Walsh doesn't do lost for words but when he says it is 'a privilege' to ride him he means it from the innermost heart. And Nicholls was all but bursting with pride, his remark 'I think that was my best ever winner' telling you exactly what this triumph meant.

We now have Kauto Star back as a major player for the rest of the season and if there is a ticket left for the rematch with Long Run at Kempton there shouldn't be.

A staying chase run next to a motorway in an unlovely neck of the Lancashire woods should not be a thing of imperishable beauty but it most palpably was exactly that. It was the day an exceptional campaigner, with every right to be feeling the passing of the years, came to Haydock, laughed at his age and bloodied the noses of the young pretenders. Three things make the great chaser – jumping, stamina and courage – and yesterday Kauto Star was flawless on all three fronts.

Here was the chaser as alchemist – turning everything into pure gold.

After the disappointing end to the previous season and the triumphant start to the new one it was time to focus attention on winning a fifth King George VI Chase, as Jon Lees reported:

Kauto Star's comeback defeat of Long Run in the Betfair Chase has put him right in contention for the King George VI Chase and forced connections to reassess their plan to limit the horse to one more start in the Cheltenham Gold Cup before he is retired.

According to owner Clive Smith, Kauto Star might not have run again until next March if he had been beaten at Haydock, but his stunning victory over the reigning champion has made a rematch with Long Run at Kempton, where he has won the Boxing Day showpiece four times, a serious option.

Despite the William Hill-sponsored race being a longstanding target for his other high-profile horse, Master Minded, Smith said it would be a shame not to give Kauto Star a chance to beat the record he shares with Desert Orchid and Nicholls said there were positive signs he could run but he would be making no commitment until he sees how well the horse comes out of Saturday's race.

'There was an original thought that maybe we should go for this race [Betfair Chase] and if he ran creditably we'd then go for the Gold Cup, but that's four months away,' said Smith. 'It may still be the best way to get the very best out of him [is to go] for one more race [the Gold Cup] and whatever happens retire him afterwards. We haven't decided on that.

'However, it seems a shame not to give him a chance in the King George. He's won it four times, he almost deserves it. It's his track, he runs it so well.

'He might have his best chance of winning the two major races of the year by going to the King George, and if he won it a fifth time it would bring the house down.'

Clifford Baker was more thrilled than most to see Kauto Star back to his imperious best at Haydock, as he told Jon Lees:

'A lot of people had written him off and you don't know in the back of your mind whether they are actually right or wrong,' he said. 'There always can be a doubt, but knowing him as well as I do I did think he was in some order.

'It all showed yesterday. We knew he could do that but to see him do it the way he did was beyond belief. I've never seen him jump better. To knock ten seconds off his own record is a fair achievement for an 11-year-old.'

Baker watched the race unfold from home with his wife Sarah and daughters Anya and Charlotte, the victory triggering a joyous family celebration in front of the television.

'We all went mad,' he said. 'There were a few tears. It was very emotional. We've all been very close to the horse forever and all we want is him safe and sound. I feel proud and privileged to work with him. I've been with him since day one. He's now won a Grade 1 for seven years on the trot which is pretty extraordinary.'

Baker said the initial signs were that Kauto Star had come out of the race encouragingly and the win had given all the staff at Ditcheat a huge lift, particularly his groom Rose Loxton who has taken over his care this season.

'He is fresh and well this morning and ate up everything. He has banners on his door. Somebody local brought in a great big box of carrots which he's probably eaten half of by now.

'The nicest moment for me last night was when he came back off the lorry and Denman, who doesn't give a monkeys about anything, neighed at him to see him back. The first thing they did was to have a sniff between the bars. It was quite a touching moment.

'He's had three different people looking after him and had success with all of them. Rose has taken him on this year after Nick Child moved on. The only other horse she does is Big Buck's and she can't believe how lucky she's been.

'The first two people to text me before and after were the two people that looked after him before, Sonja and Nick. He'll always be as big a part of their lives as he is ours.'

In winning a fourth Betfair Chase, Kauto Star set a new record, as racing historian John Randall wrote:

Kauto Star is the only horse ever to win two different Group/Grade 1 races four times each.

The greatest steeplechaser since Arkle is unique in winning the King George VI Chase four consecutive times (2006-09), and the Betfair Chase at Haydock, which he landed for the fourth time on

Clive Smith sports a 'Kauto Star' tie and badge at Kempton Park on Boxing Day 2011

Saturday, has also had Grade 1 status since its inaugural running in 2005.

Kauto Star has won a total of 15 Grade 1 races, has triumphed at that level in seven different seasons and has earned £2,272,891 in prize money. All those are records for a jumper trained in Britain or Ireland.

This is in addition to being officially the best steeplechaser in all three distance categories – 2m, 2m4f and 3m-plus – in 2006-07, and the only horse ever to regain his Cheltenham Gold Cup crown.

Before Kauto Star, Istabraq was the horse who went closest to winning two different Group/Grade 1 races four times each.

Aidan O'Brien's star won two prizes at Leopardstown – the local Champion Hurdle and the December Festival Hurdle – four times between 1997 and 2001.

Both are now Grade 1, but at the time the December Festival Hurdle had only Grade 2 status; it was not promoted to the top level until 2002.

Kauto went into the King George for the first time as underdog, but Paul Nicholls had him back in fine form after the problems of the previous season. He wowed the Boxing Day crowd with an emotional win that put the horse in the hearts of racing fans everywhere, as Jon Lees reported:

Great British sporting achievement is measured in fives and yesterday racing rejoiced in the equine equivalent of Sir Steve Redgrave, the five-time Olympic gold medallist, after Kauto Star pulled off an extraordinary feat of his own by winning the William Hill King George VI Chase for a fifth time.

At the track where a statue stands of four-time winner Desert Orchid, Kauto Star demonstrated he belonged on a different plinth when he beat the record he shared with the great grey at Kempton Park by completing a resounding Boxing Day victory over Long Run.

A rivalry that appeared to be one-sided at the end of last season when the five years younger Long Run captured both the King George and the Cheltenham Gold Cup is now evenly balanced after Kauto Star levelled the match score to two victories each, while the prospect of retirement for Paul Nicholls' chasing giant, a keen topic of discussion in the summer, is as far away as ever.

Old age is not having the impact on Kauto Star that it does on lesser horses as Clive Smith's 11-year-old produced a dominant display to beat Long Run by a length-and-a-quarter margin that in no way reflected his comprehensive mastery of his young rival.

By leading the race out from as early as the eighth of the 18 fences, jockey Ruby Walsh sought to put pressure on Long Run well before the field reached the straight. While Long Run's jumping became ragged, Kauto Star's was impeccable as he turned for home needing only to maintain momentum to land the spoils.

Long Run fought up the straight but a mistake at the last put paid to any chance of victory as Kauto Star crossed the line to spark joyous scenes among the near 21,000 crowd.

Walsh, standing up in the irons waving his whip in celebration, saluted the ecstatic stands by parading back in front of them before returning to the winner's enclosure where they were greeted by a jubilant Nicholls and Smith.

'That was awesome,' said the trainer. 'I knew we had him right. He was going so well at home and looked fantastic. I didn't really believe this was possible but when he ran at Haydock and then on what I have seen since I thought yes it was.

'He was never right last season and with hindsight I think it took him a while to get over that fall in last year's Gold Cup. Ruby is a

KEMPTON, 26 December 2011		
William Hill King George VI Chase		3m
1 Kauto Star	3-1	R Walsh
2 Long Run	evensf	Mr S Waley-Cohen
3 Captain Chris	8-1	R Johnson
7 ran 1¼l, 17l		

massive plus because he knows him so well and when he is right like that he is still as good as ever. He's come in and he's not even having a blow. He was like that at Haydock. Last year he bled here and was out on his feet.

'It just shows what a great horse he is and how good he is for racing. This is why people keep coming back and why jump racing is so popular. Six times he has been here and five times he has won. I will never have another like him. A chaser like that is astounding.'

Smith said: 'I am so proud. He just seems better than ever. He is an extraordinary horse. I'll never have one like him in my lifetime again.'

Kauto Star, who turns 12 on Sunday, was cut to 9-2 from 10-1 for the Gold Cup by William Hill but Long Run remains favourite at 3-1 from 5-2. Kauto Star is 4-1 second favourite with Ladbrokes and Coral.

Nicholls added: 'A lot of people wrote him off at the beginning of the season and now he has come back at 11 and won two Grade 1 races. If we can get him in really good shape he will run really well at Cheltenham.

'He's got to be the one to beat. Forget his age – on his two runs this year he is the horse in form. He finished weakly in the Gold Cup, but the way he's finishing now he'll be fine. The way he is going he doesn't want retiring. He's in too good shape. His star is still burning bright.'

Walsh, who missed the last King George through injury, feared Long Run would improve a lot for the Betfair Chase where he was beaten by a fitter Kauto Star.

'Long Run was exceptional last year both here and in the Gold Cup,' he said.

'Maybe we caught him on the hop at Haydock and I was thinking he was going to be a better horse today.

'I took the view that Long Run had won a Gold Cup but never a Tingle Creek and I was riding the quicker horse. The weak don't last in any walk of life and that's why he is so brilliant.'

Alastair Down revelled in an occasion those lucky enough to witness would never forget:

On an afternoon that reached far into the soul, Kauto Star propelled himself into territory where he now stands gloriously alone as the only five-time winner of the King George after a victory that shivered the spine and quivered many a voice shouting happy acclaim.

Increasingly a marvel beyond measure, there was something spellbinding and contagiously irresistible about watching Kauto Star and Ruby Walsh lording it flagrantly from the front with more than a circuit to run, the man on top utterly confident in the might and magic of the horse beneath.

And of course the Kempton crowd, many of whom had made the journey with one heartfelt wish uppermost in their mind, picked up the vibe that they were ringside to racing history. Even those who had helped lever Long Run into short-priced favouritism must have given up the unequal struggle and surrendered to the magnificence of the sight in front of them and added their voices to the uproar.

From fully six fences out, where Long Run was far from fluent, the call went out from the stands as the crowd passed simmer and hit boil. There was a solid blast of sound and transmission of will as they roared their encouragement for the horse who had four times

'I wish I had him. He's a fantastic horse and it's great for racing. I wasn't surprised how well he did it because he ran a blinder at Haydock.'

Jonjo O'Neill, leading trainer

Kauto Star on his way to an historic Kempton triumph, 26 December 2011

delivered on this day and from whom they so fervently wanted a fifth – not for themselves but for the horse himself.

As they turned in with three to jump, in front of countless televisions up and down the land, voices must also have been raised to happy frenzy and chairs emptied as folk rose to their feet to better absorb the moving image and add their pound of vocal flesh to the clamour beseeching Kauto Star and the sporting gods that he would stay in front.

Kauto Star was nothing less than magnificent up this straight, measuring its three trappy fences with total assurance. It was after he had soared over three out that you knew in your grateful heart that he wasn't going to be denied and you felt able to let yourself go with the flow of the fantastic reception as the whole course joyfully erupted on his run down to the second-last.

Once again he was foot perfect and the wall of sound mounted to another level that proceeded to go off the scale when Kauto and Ruby cleared the last and galloped towards the line. Long Run tried

Ruby Walsh celebrates at Kempton with Long Run defeated

courageously to grind him down but the margin of a mere length and a quarter should not mislead anyone into thinking this was ever in doubt.

As far as the jumps faithful were concerned, once the post was passed all heaven broke loose. Right across the stands and enclosures the applause crashed out. This was not the polite putting together of paws at tummy level but the mass adulatory smash of hands being bought together over head height, the very stuff of acclaim. As Walsh brought him back before the people – Kauto Star's people – racegoers pressed down to the rails to be closer to the two heroes of so many hours and now of this indelible one as well.

The cheering never dropped a decibel and the laughter never died, a huge collective smile was painted over thousands of faces and if there were heads shaking from side to side it was in simple awe and gratitude. All the way back round towards the winner's enclosure Kauto Star's every step was met by a symphony of cheers from men and women who knew they had witnessed something beyond price from a horse who, by any reckoning, must be considered one of the two greatest chasers of the post-war era.

Somehow in Kauto Star all the essential qualities come together and his class is underpinned by frontline courage. Time was, years ago, when he would throw in the odd mistake but this season he has jumped all but flawlessly and he still races with an exuberance that is captivating given that he is almost 12 years old. He must love this game as much as we enjoy watching him.

There was a sense of wonder in the air at Kempton yesterday and it was a total pleasure to be swept up by it. There is something powerful and unifying about sharing with your fellow human beings something that is pure celebration. I saw some tough customers struggling and then surrendering to the sheer emotional force of the moment, but doing so with faces every bit as blissful as they were tearful.

In the immediate afterglow of this King George is perhaps not the time to draw lofty conclusions about Kauto Star's exact place in the pantheon. But two things can not be gainsaid: Kauto Star has on his honour roll achievements over trips that do not appear on the rightly immortal Arkle's winning record and he has been at the top for

'There's no question now, he's the best there's been since Arkle. He beat a King George winner and a Gold Cup winner and the form of the race stacks up. I couldn't have been more impressed.'

Johnny Lumley, Arkle's groom

'Kauto is an absolute star. I always think that in attempting to evaluate horses one ought to leave Arkle out of the equation because he was a complete freak, but Kauto is right up there with any of the other outstanding horses who have won this race.'

Sir Peter O'Sullevan, the Voice of Racing

Kauto Star is led around the winner's enclosure at Kempton by Rose Loxton

seven successive seasons in which he has won Grade 1 races, another colossal attribute to which Arkle has no answer. Although perhaps he does not need one.

If you need an illustration of Kauto Star's potent longevity then ponder on the fact that he won his first British steeplechase before yesterday's runner-up Long Run was born.

Deeds such as Kauto Star's fifth King George are among the defining moments of sporting lifetimes. I never saw Arkle triumph but I have seen Kauto Star win plenty of races and no passage of time will ever decrease my undying gratitude for that very genuine blessing.

In scenes Ditcheat was so familiar with, Kauto Star returned home the following day to a hero's reception, as Jon Lees reported:

Kauto Star may go into the 2012 Betfred Cheltenham Gold Cup as an underdog but trainer Paul Nicholls yesterday warned that his record-breaking chaser would ask more serious questions of Long Run in March than he did when only third in this year's race.

Even though Kauto Star will turn 12 in three days' time, Nicholls sees no reason why the dual Gold Cup winner can't sustain the form he has shown in defeating Long Run in both the William Hill King George VI Chase and Betfair Chase.

Kauto Star is paraded through Ditcheat by Clifford Baker and Rose Loxton

'The King George took a lot out of him last season,' Nicholls said. 'He was finishing his races quite tamely, whereas this season he is back to the top of his game. He is a different horse form-wise. I have no idea why but he is. He has almost turned the clock back. Going into the Gold Cup you want to be judging him on this season's form, not last season's Gold Cup run.

'There's no reason why he can't keep this up until March given the form he's in. We can keep him like this now, we've done it a few times. We can get him in this form for March and we are looking forward to the challenge.'

Kauto Star is a best-priced 5-1 with Betfred for the Gold Cup after collecting his fifth King George on Monday over Long Run, who is 5-2 favourite with the sponsors and a best-priced 3-1 with Ladbrokes and William Hill.

'On this season's form the Gold Cup will be totally different to last season,' Nicholls said. 'Long Run is probably still favourite because he will be seven and there is an uphill finish, but Kauto Star has won two Gold Cups and it never worried him. I still think he is slightly better left-handed.

'If he was eight he probably would be favourite but I don't mind if we go into the race underdog again. Long Run is a good horse but he is having a few hard races and it will be a test of his constitution to see if he can keep bouncing back from them. I know Kauto will.

'Kauto was obviously way better than last season [in the King George]. I don't think the form of last season's race is anyway near Kauto's performance on Monday. He jumped and galloped and put it up to Long Run. Last season Nacarat and Riverside Theatre [second and fourth in the King George] were just too close to him and he didn't perform to anywhere near his best.'

Kauto Star recovered well enough to take to the roads of Ditcheat yesterday. He was welcomed by one of the biggest crowds he has ever attracted to the Manor House Inn, from where he began a parade through his home village.

'I couldn't believe how many people and camera crews were outside the pub an hour before he was due to parade,' Nicholls said. 'The whole thing has been fantastic. You would hardly know Kauto Star has had a race.

'He is about to have a flu jab, which all of our horses get at this time of year. Then he will have a couple of quiet weeks. We will keep him ticking over and he will probably canter every day from the middle of January until early February and then we will start getting him back in the full routine and work him hard up to the Gold Cup.'

At the beginning of February Nicholls said his chasing legend was back to his best in the build-up to the Gold Cup. Ben Newton went to visit:

Paul Nicholls yesterday reported Kauto Star in stunning condition as he steps up his preparation for a sixth consecutive appearance in the Gold Cup and a fifth clash with arch-rival Long Run at Cheltenham six weeks today.

The 12-year-old chasing legend came out of his record-breaking fifth King George win 'so fresh we didn't have to give him any time off'.

The trainer said: 'He had an easy ten days after his flu jab at the beginning of January and hasn't missed a beat since. He's done his two canters up the hill with Clifford this morning and looks fantastic – in stunning condition.

'It's just like old times with him; you wouldn't know he'd had two hardish races in top company. He just keeps on astounding me.

Those two victories this season have given him so much confidence that he believes in himself again. Without doubt he's back to his best and now we're aiming to keep him that way in the run-up to Cheltenham.'

Kauto Star's return to top form is a far cry from last season when, despite winning at Down Royal and being placed in the King George and Gold Cup, he was not finishing his races, according to Nicholls.

'My assistant Dan Skelton has a fair point when he says he reckons it took Kauto a full season to get over the very heavy fall he had in the 2010 Gold Cup, from which he was lucky to escape with his life,' said Nicholls.

'And there were other factors: the interruptions with the weather, and the postponed King George, meant he was not in his usual routine, and he thrives on routine.

'Then there was the change of jockey in the King George. I say this with absolutely no disrespect to AP [McCoy], but Kauto and Ruby are a match made in heaven. All these things made a difference last season.'

Kauto Star's final run, when pulled up at Punchestown last spring, led to increasing calls for his retirement, but his trainer said: 'I rely on my own judgement and work things out in accordance with the wishes of Clive Smith, and I was quietly confident he would come back and win a fourth Betfair Chase. But what he's done this season is phenomenal for a horse now 12.'

After the two defeats Kauto Star has inflicted on 2011 Gold Cup winner Long Run, Nicholls reckons bookmakers may have it wrong in making Long Run 9-4 favourite to defend the Betfred-sponsored chasing classic on March 16.

'You can argue Kauto deserves to be Gold Cup favourite,' he said, 'and if he were eight instead of 12 he would be. At the very least he and Long Run probably deserve to be joint-favourites. But the one thing about this year's race is the top two are miles clear of anything else on form. As we've seen in the past, no race is a two-horse race unless there are only two runners.

'I'll respect Grands Crus, of course, if they decide to go there, but to me he is the horse we have to beat in next season's King George and Gold Cup.

Kauto Star with Paul Nicholls

Kauto Star, held by Clifford Baker,
with Paul Nicholls (front) and (back
from left) Dan Skelton, Donna Blake
and Rose Loxton

'I'm sure Nicky [Henderson] will fancy his chances of turning Kempton form around as Cheltenham will suit his horse much better, but I'm not certain Long Run has improved this season like most people expected him to.

'He had plenty of hard races in France as a youngster and it may be he has already reached a plateau. Kauto and Ruby are such a lethal weapon right now that Long Run is going to have to pull something out to turn the tables.

'And remember, sad though it is, Denman is retired, so this year Kauto won't have him pressurising him as he goes to the top of the hill at Cheltenham.'

The six-time champion trainer is adamant he has been able to train Kauto Star harder this season than at any point in his career, and promised: 'From now on we'll get some real graft into him. Last week his routine was one canter up our hill on Monday, two on Tuesday, one on Wednesday, two on Thursday and so on; this week he's been up there twice every morning and next week we'll step him up further. And the way he looks he'll be turning up at Cheltenham in much better shape than he did 12 months ago.'

Nicholls said if Kauto Star can regain his crown for a second time and become the first of his age since What A Myth in 1969 to win the Gold Cup, it would be 'simply unbelievable'.

And he added that as long as his star acquits himself well, there is unlikely to be talk of retirement. 'You don't even think about drawing stumps with a horse at the top of his game,' he said. 'In his current form there's no reason why he can't come back next season and run in another Betfair Chase and King George – provided that's what Clive wants to do.'

Looking back on the horse's unforgettable triumph at Kempton over Christmas, Nicholls said: 'The enormity of it still hasn't sunk in over a month later, and the scenes outside the pub the following day will live with me forever. It will be a sad day when he's no longer in his box. When you have to say goodbye to the horse of a lifetime it's going to leave a huge hole in all our lives.'

After what had been a trouble-free preparation since his record-breaking King George victory on Boxing Day, Paul Nicholls shocked the racing world two weeks before the festival showpiece when he

Kauto Star and Clifford Baker at Manor Farm Stables

announced that Kauto Star had taken an 'awful' fall while being schooled by Ruby Walsh at home on February 24. James Pugh reported:

The clash between the resurgent Kauto Star and reigning Gold Cup hero Long Run was hanging in the balance last night after trainer Paul Nicholls revealed his stable star had taken an 'awful' fall in a schooling session at Ditcheat last week and is only 50-50 to make the Cheltenham highlight in a fortnight's time.

Racing fans will be on tenterhooks in the lead-up to Cheltenham as Nicholls said Kauto Star's progress next week would be crucial to his prospects of making the Gold Cup line-up.

Bookmakers reacted swiftly to the news, with BetVictor offering a top-priced 9-2 about Kauto Star and, along with Ladbrokes, going as short as evens about Long Run retaining his crown. Betfred also cut the David Pipe-trained Grands Crus to 6-1 (from 8) with connections still undecided whether to run in the RSA Chase or take on more experienced rivals in the Gold Cup.

Announcing the news, Nicholls said yesterday: 'Kauto took a tumble when Ruby schooled him at the end of last week. I say tumble, but in truth it was a pretty awful fall.

'Clive was obviously consulted at all times and we immediately got Kauto checked over. Even though he trotted sound, it was plain to see he was sore afterwards. He's had the best veterinary and physiotherapy care possible but we hoped he would be showing more improvement by now.'

Nicholls, writing in his Betfair column, continued: 'I spoke to Clifford after returning to the stables after a Cheltenham media day on Wednesday, and he said Kauto still wasn't fully recovered, remained quite stiff, and in his wise words he felt he was 'only 50-50' to make the festival at this stage.

'So I immediately spoke to Clive and we felt it prudent that we put out this update today.'

Nicholls did provide some hope to Kauto Star's legion of followers when stating: 'One thing I think we've all learned with Kauto is never to write him off.

'Yes, having this setback so close to the festival is clearly a major concern, but don't confuse Kauto's kind and inquisitive nature with softness.

'He's a hard so-and-so too – you learn to be when your best mate is Denman – and it wouldn't surprise me in the slightest if he was back firing on all cylinders at home before Cheltenham and went on to beat Long Run for a third time this season.'

Kauto Star, who regained the Gold Cup in 2009, finished third to Long Run in the Gold Cup last season but exacted revenge on his younger rival with a thrilling victory in the Betfair Chase at Haydock before again denying him when storming to a fifth King George VI Chase at Kempton in December.

Smith, speaking to the *Racing Post* last night, said: 'I'm devastated about the whole thing. Kauto Star is fine in himself, but he's bruised and probably stretched one or two muscles he might not have wanted to.

'He's in very good hands, of course. The whole team down at Ditcheat are working on him giving him treatment and massages and Buffy [Shirley-Beavan], the vet, is really looking after him along with Clifford Baker and Paul Nicholls. We're just trying to get him right and we'll see how he comes on.

'He was in the schooling ring and he just touched one of his jumps, took a tumble and went down. I was standing three or four yards away. It was very sad.'

Smith added: 'I just don't know if he'll make the Gold Cup, I've got to take the advice of the experts – the vets. I've got to see whether he's right. If he's not right on the day, we can't run him as I wouldn't want anything to happen to him because he's not quite fit enough or not quite himself.

'I want him to run, obviously. I'd love him to, but you can't run him unless he's absolutely right. The horse's health is much more important.'

Reflecting on the announcement, Smith added: 'It only happened on Friday but equally we were just trying to see whether it was serious or not.

'The vet couldn't put any spot on it at the time and it's just unfortunate it's happened. I'm just taking the advice given to me, but it's a shame it perhaps hasn't come out earlier.

'There was no good warning everybody unless there was something to warn them about, and we just didn't know how he would recover day by day.'

Walsh, speaking on Racing UK, said: 'It was pretty routine and he was in great form but unfortunately he miscalculated going towards the last jump and fell quite heavily.

'He's probably been around that school 1,000 times. It's unfortunate and it's a worry, but it is what it is. Horses fall, that's part of racing. Unfortunately it's not great timing, but it happened.

'I didn't see him after. I'm only the jockey. The people at Ditcheat look after him.'

He added: 'They just don't think he's right. It's the Gold Cup and you can't go there half-cocked. They are just letting people know.

'It's two weeks away yet. A lot can happen in 24 hours in a horse's life, let alone two weeks. As Paul said, it's 50-50 and a lot will depend on what happens in the next ten days. If he's right he'll run, if he's not he won't.'

There were almost daily bulletins from Ditcheat as to the wellbeing of the two-time Gold Cup hero, and each day brought more positive updates. Paul Nicholls declared Kauto Star was ready to run although he did not expect a fairytale third success.

The 2012 Gold Cup started promisingly for Kauto Star, but on the first circuit it quickly became apparent that he was not quite right and, Ruby Walsh pulled him up before Synchronised triumphed under a superb ride from Tony McCoy.

David Carr reported:

Owner Clive Smith all but admitted Kauto Star has run the last race of a memorable career after his outstanding chaser was pulled up on the first circuit in his sixth crack at the Betfred Cheltenham Gold Cup.

The dual winner was up with the pace early on but lost his place after clearing the water jump and was trailing the field when Ruby Walsh called it a day before the tenth – to applause from the packed stands.

Kauto Star, whose participation had been in doubt after a schooling fall, was sound when he returned to the unsaddling enclosure. But asked whether he would be retired, Smith said: 'There will be no snap decision but I am 90 per cent sure.

'I will take advice but someone will have to work very hard to persuade me that we should see him out again because what I wouldn't want to happen is have a Best Mate situation or a Dawn Run. I don't want anything like that, I'd just rather call it a day maybe.

'We'll see how we go and we will talk about it. It's a very sad occasion really because it will be the last time probably we will see him on the track.'

Trainer Paul Nicholls deflected a question about retirement and said: 'Let's not worry about that for the minute, he's been a blinding horse and we'll turn him away in the summer and see what happens.'

Reflecting on Kauto Star's early departure, Smith said: 'He jumped the first two or three fences and Ruby felt very happy with him, but when he got to the water jump he had to stretch a bit and that was where he felt some internal pain somewhere and Ruby could feel he was dropping back straight away. His instructions had been to pull him up if he was not right.

'He's not seriously injured at all. It's like getting a tweak in the back playing golf, it's a little minor injury that caused him some pain and he couldn't go on.'

Walsh said: 'With the greatest respect to the horses concerned, Midnight Chase, Time For Rupert and Knockara Beau are not quick enough for Kauto Star when he's right and they were able to go faster than me.

'He felt great last Friday and Monday but it's not until you ask them the question that you know, and you can't ask those questions at home because you have to keep a bit for the race.

'I was thinking about pulling up when AP said "If I were you I'd be pulling up". It would have been a hell of a lot worse if I'd turned him over and he'd broken his neck.'

Nicholls added: 'We had an injury a fortnight ago, we've done our best and I said to Ruby "if you're in any doubt pull him up". The most important thing today was that he came back all right.

'He's not lame but obviously something is not right. You can't tell – Clifford Baker rode him work two days ago and said there

Following spread: Kauto Star and Ruby Walsh remain the focus, as the rest of the Gold Cup field continue on the first circuit, 16 March 2012

CHELTENHAM, 16 March 2012			
Betfred Cheltenham Gold Cup Chase		3m21/2f	
1	Synchronised	8-1	AP McCoy
2	The Giant Bolster	50-1	T Scudamore
3	Long Run	7-4f	Mr S Waley-Cohen
PU	Kauto Star	3-1	R Walsh
14 ran 21/4l, 3/4l			

Dan Skelton greets the wounded hero

was absolutely nothing wrong with him. But you can't replicate the pressure of a race.'

Kauto Star was bidding for a 17th Grade 1 victory yesterday and Smith added: 'I will look back on a wonderful career. He has been a fantastic horse, I couldn't have wished for a better horse.'

At the end of May it was announced that Kauto Star was the highest rated jumper for the fourth time, as Graham Dench reported:

Kauto Star has been recognised as the highest-rated jumper for a fourth time in six seasons with an end-of-season mark of 180, a remarkable achievement for a 12-year-old who had pretty much been written off at this time last year.

While 180 falls 10lb short of the figure he achieved two seasons ago, it puts him 2lb in front of Long Run, from whom he regained the title, with ill-fated Gold Cup winner Synchronised and now-retired Grand National winner Neptune Collonges heading the remainder in the 3m+ category a further 10lb behind.

Kauto Star has no fewer than seven Anglo-Irish titles to his name and, while a decision has yet to be made on his future, head of handicapping Phil Smith is in no doubt about his status within the sport.

Smith, who spoke of a 'huge void' at the top of the chasing tree if Kauto Star joins Denman in retirement and Imperial Commander struggles to return to his best, said: 'Kauto Star is undoubtedly the best chaser we have seen on these shores in many a long year and to have put up 22 performances rated 170+ is absolutely stunning.

'Apart from his level of performance, his consistency is fantastic and he is still the only horse who has ever been champion at two miles, two and a half miles and three miles in the same season.

'I thought Haydock might be his last hurrah and I expected Long Run to get his revenge at Kempton, but he beat Long Run again and there's no question that was another 180+ performance. There were issues before Cheltenham, but we had an Istabraq moment when he received a great reception after pulling up.'

Trainer Paul Nicholls said: 'That rating puts in perspective how good he's been. To come back and win those two races and the King

George for a fifth time was fantastic. They were two performances out of the very top drawer to beat last year's Gold Cup winner. It was such a shame he had that little incident before Cheltenham. He was in such good form at the time.

'As he is now, he is rated higher this season at grass than he was this time last year. He is out at grass with Big Buck's and looks fantastic. He was cantering away at the end of the season and is fine.

'I haven't got together with Clive to make any decision. We'll do that later.'

As Britain basked in the success of the Olympic Games and the racing world turned its focus to the mighty Frankel, Kauto Star spent the summer months of 2012 in the fields of Somerset with his old friend and former rival Denman – which is where, with gratitude for his unforgettable career, we leave the greatest steeplechaser of the modern era.

The racing record

KAUTO STAR (FR)

* bay gelding foaled 19 March 2000
* Village Star (Fr) - Kauto Relka (Fr) (Port Etienne (Fr))
* Breeder Mme Henri Aubert

Date	Course	Going	Race name (pattern status in parentheses)	Distance in furlongs	Jockey	Starting price	Finishing position	Prize money in pounds sterling
2002/03								
1 Mar	Bordeaux	good	Prix Bournosienne	15	F Barrao		2nd	
14 Apr	Enghien	very soft	Prix du Brevent	15	F Barrao		1st	£11,221
2003/04								
4 May	Auteuil	very soft	Prix Go Ahead	15	F Barrao		1st	£12,468
27 Sep	Auteuil	very soft	Prix Robert Lejeune (Listed)	18	J Guiheneuf		1st	£20,260
11 Oct	Auteuil	very soft	Prix Georges de Talhouet-Roy (Gr2)	18	J Guiheneuf		F	
2 Nov	Auteuil	very soft	Prix Cambaceres (Gr2)	18	J Guiheneuf		2nd	£30,000
7 Mar	Auteuil	soft	Prix Jacques d'Indy (Gr3)	18	J Guiheneuf		3rd	£10,986
27 Mar	Auteuil	very soft	Prix de Pepinvast (Gr3)	18	J Guiheneuf		5th	£4,225
24 Apr	Auteuil	very soft	Prix Amadou (Gr2)	20	J Guiheneuf		3rd	£13,732
2004/05								
30 May	Auteuil	very soft	Gras Savoye Vie et Avenir Prix de Longchamp (Gr3)	20	J Guiheneuf	36-1	1st	£38,028
29 Dec	Newbury	good to soft	Western Daily Press Club Novices' Chase	19	R Walsh	2-1JF	1st	£8,840
31 Jan	Exeter	soft	Weatherbys Bank Novices' Chase	18	R Walsh	2-11F	2nd	£2,477
2005/06								
1 Nov	Exeter	good to soft	William Hill Haldon Gold Cup Chase (Gr2)	18	R Walsh	3-1	2nd	£13,903.50
3 Dec	Sandown Park	soft	William Hill - Tingle Creek Chase (Gr1)	16	M Fitzgerald	5-2JF	1st	£71,275
15 Mar	Cheltenham	good	Queen Mother Champion Chase (Gr1)	16	R Walsh	2-1F	F	
2006/07								
22 Oct	Aintree	good	Bonusprint.com Old Roan Chase (Gr2)	20	R Walsh	evens F	1st	£28,510
18 Nov	Haydock Park	good to soft	Betfair Chase (Gr1)	24	R Walsh	11-10F	1st	£114,040
2 Dec	Sandown Park	soft	William Hill – Tingle Creek Chase (Gr1)	16	R Walsh	4-9F	1st	£79,828

Date	Course	Going	Race		Jockey	Price	Position	Prize
26 Dec	Kempton Park	good to soft	Stan James King George VI Chase (Gr1)	24	R Walsh	8-13F	1st	£114,040
10 Feb	Newbury	soft	Aon Chase (Gr2)	24	R Walsh	2-9F	1st	£28,510
16 Mar	Cheltenham	good to soft	Totesport Cheltenham Gold Cup Chase (Gr1)	27	R Walsh	5-4F	1st	£242,335

2007/08

Date	Course	Going	Race		Jockey	Price	Position	Prize
28 Oct	Aintree	good	Bonusprint.com Old Roan Chase (Gr2)	20	R Walsh	11-10F	2nd	£11,585
24 Nov	Haydock Park	soft	Betfair Chase (Gr1)	24	S Thomas	4-5F	1st	£114,040
26 Dec	Kempton Park	good to soft	Stan James King George VI Chase (Gr1)	24	R Walsh	4-6F	1st	£126,033.60
16 Feb	Ascot	good	Commercial First Ascot Chase (Gr1)	22	R Walsh	4-11F	1st	£84,510
14 Mar	Cheltenham	good to soft	Totesport Cheltenham Gold Cup Chase (Gr1)	27	R Walsh	10-11F	2nd	£100,639.95
3 Apr	Aintree	good	Totesport Bowl Chase (Gr2)	25	R Walsh	4-7F	2nd	£34,224

2008/09

Date	Course	Going	Race		Jockey	Price	Position	Prize
1 Nov	Down Royal	soft	JNWine.com Champion Chase (Gr1)	24	R Walsh	2-5F	1st	£66,911.76
22 Nov	Haydock Park	good to soft	Betfair Chase (Gr1)	24	S Thomas	2-5F	UR	
26 Dec	Kempton Park	good	Stan James King George VI Chase (Gr1)	24	R Walsh	10-11F	1st	£130,648.03
13 Mar	Cheltenham	good to soft	Totesport Cheltenham Gold Cup Chase (Gr1)	27	R Walsh	7-4F	1st	£270,797.50

2009/10

Date	Course	Going	Race		Jockey	Price	Position	Prize
21 Nov	Haydock Park	soft	Betfair Chase (Gr1)	24	R Walsh	4-6F	1st	£112,660
26 Dec	Kempton Park	good to soft	William King George VI Chase (Gr1)	24	R Walsh	8-13F	1st	£114,020
19 Mar	Cheltenham	good	Totesport Cheltenham Gold Cup Chase (Gr1)	27	R Walsh	8-11F	F	

2010/11

Date	Course	Going	Race		Jockey	Price	Position	Prize
6 Nov	Down Royal	soft	JNWine.com Champion Chase (Gr1)	24	R Walsh	4-7F	1st	£74,336.28
15 Jan	Kempton Park	good to soft	William Hill King George VI Chase (Gr1)	24	AP McCoy	4-7F	3rd	£19,278
18 Mar	Cheltenham	good	Totesport Cheltenham Gold Cup Chase (Gr1)	27	R Walsh	5-1	3rd	£53,550

2011/12

Date	Course	Going	Race		Jockey	Price	Position	Prize
4 May	Punchestown	good	Punchestown Guinness Gold Cup (Gr1)	25	R Walsh	10-11F	PU	
19 Nov	Haydock Park	good to soft	Betfair Chase (Gr1)	24	R Walsh	6-1	1st	£113,072
26 Dec	Kempton Park	good to soft	William Hill King George VI Chase (Gr1)	24	R Walsh	3-1	1st	£102,992.40
16 Mar	Cheltenham	good, good to soft in places	Betfred Cheltenham Gold Cup Chase (Gr1)	27	R Walsh	3-1	PU	

KAUTO STAR

- raced 41 times, winning 23 times
- earned £2,375,883 in prize money in Britain, Ireland and France
- longest price in Britain: 6-1 in 2011 Betfair Chase
- shortest price in Britain: 2-11 in 2005 Western Daily Press Club Novices' Chase
- longest winning distance: 36 lengths in 2009 William Hill King George VI Chase
- shortest winning distance: nose in 2009 Betfair Chase
- only failed to complete six times

Index

Overleaf: Kauto Star and Ruby Walsh winning the Betfair Chase, November 2011